The Science of Overcoming Procrastination:
How to Be Disciplined, Break Inertia, Manage Your Time, and Be Productive. Get Off Your Butt and Get Things Done!

By Patrick King
Social Interaction Specialist and
Conversation Coach
www.PatrickKingConsulting.com

Table of Contents

Introduction

I want to start this book with a story about procrastination, but maybe I'll tell you tomorrow...

When my mother was pregnant with me, my father promised to build a shelf in my nursery room to house all the keepsakes and memorabilia I would create as a growing human being. For instance, locks of hair from my first haircut, my baby teeth when they fell out, my first fingernail clippings, the bracelet that was put on me right after I was born, and my first pair of shoes. It seems like everything parents keep of their children is some form of refuse or garbage, but I suppose the sentimental value can't be discounted. The shelf was also supposed to have space across the top and bottom to act as a photo album, along with a ruler running down one side to track my height.

Sounds like a pretty good idea, right? Cute, even. At least, that's what my father thought.

He conceived of this idea when I was barely the size of a peanut, which would place my mother somewhere between two and four months of pregnancy, roughly. The shelf ended up being built after I had already lost my first tooth, which would place me at roughly seven years old.

His grand shelf had a turnaround time of almost eight years, and it can probably be assumed that he wasn't off searching the world for the perfect tree to harvest wood from. It is also rather unlikely that he had changed his mind and wanted to wait for me to grow up so we could share the experience of building something together, though it's an excuse that sounds as good as any.

He just procrastinated and never quite got around it. It always remained on his to-do list, but other tasks seemed to take precedence over it or have greater urgency. I later asked him how he allowed this to happen, and he said that it simply seemed like too big of a task and that everything else seemed easier to complete, so he would just perform those tasks first—washing the car, cleaning the gutters, cooking a pie. He might not have enjoyed any of those tasks, but at least they were relatively small, had a definite ending time, and he knew exactly where he could start.

Naturally, the next question I had was what motivated him to finally set his sights on finishing the shelf. It was completely related to his reason for not starting. Instead of viewing a shelf as an insurmountable task that would take up weeks of his time, he began to view it as something to do little by little. And he took this to the highest degree, buying some nails one weekend, taking some measurements another, and buying 1-2 pieces of the required lumber each month.

In other words, he took it slow and broke the overwhelming task into tiny steps that ultimately made it easy to say, "Oh, what the heck, I can do this right now." Despite my father's six years of delay tactics and absentmindedness, this is a story about how to slay the procrastination beast in a way we can all implement in our daily lives.

One of the biggest weapons you have against procrastination is its natural enemy: making tasks almost impossible to skip over in the present moment. We'll cover that in more detail later.

Perhaps it is hereditary, but procrastination has also plagued me for years in both my personal and professional life. I'm embarrassed to say that I pulled multiple all-nighters in college and never seemed to learn my lesson. Breaking tasks into tiny steps was a big factor in defeating it, but understanding the psychology behind procrastination and why we can't seem to do what's best for us is what will really get you to where you want to be.

Humans are many things, but acting in a way that is consistent with our intentions is not something we specialize in. It's time to dig deep into what happens in our brains when we suddenly want to clean the bathroom to avoid our homework. You might find more than you bargained for, but the end goal will always be the same: you'll be able to get off your butt and accomplish your goals on a consistent basis.

Procrastination will hopefully be relegated to a distant memory instead of a constant battle.

Chapter 1. Procrastination: The Ancient Foe

"Procrastination is opportunity's assassin."
- Victor Kiam

If you've chosen to read this book, you may have met procrastination before. It probably needs no introduction, especially when you've known it all your life. Since the moment you were old enough to recognize that you actually have to option to build a Lego castle rather than sit down to do your math homework, procrastination has been there in the background, encouraging you to do that what is worst for you. It's like your shadow; you just can't shake it, it's always with you, and it's easy to forget about.

But unlike your shadow, it's deadset on ruining your life!

Now you're stuck with it and having problems because it's starting to control you, like one of those relationships which started out fun but has grown to ruin almost every aspect of your life. You want to break up with it to get your life back on track, but you don't know how to.

Well, the answer in knowing how to finally get back in control from the demoralizing domination of procrastination is in this book. It starts with getting to really know procrastination for what it truly is, and the many faces it shows when tricking you to hand over the reins to it again.

What is procrastination?

The term "procrastination" was derived from the Latin *pro*, meaning "forward, forth, or in favor of," and *crastinus*, meaning "of tomorrow." Its literal translation can thus be taken to be the moving forward of something to tomorrow, or favoring tomorrow as the ideal time. It's never today; always another moment to be later determined.

Procrastination is the act or habit of putting off something to a future time. It involves delaying what needs to be done, usually because the task is unpleasant or boring— or simply because delaying is an option. It's typically considered an exclusively negative phenomenon, involving some degree of psychological discomfort and/or irrationality. For example, the thought of having to write out a three-chapter research proposal brings psychological discomfort, so you may delay working on the task for as long as you can. You may also simply have some extra time and want to watch a movie instead.

The next thing you know, you've put off writing the proposal until it's just a day before the deadline—which wasn't exactly a rational move, given the sheer size of workload involved and the shortness of time you now have to complete it. Rationality isn't involved in procrastinating; in fact, rationality is used far less on a daily basis than we would like to think. And thus, we find ourselves in a hole of our own digging.

Note that procrastination deals only with intended tasks (i.e. tasks you should be doing), and not all *the other tasks* open for you to do. For instance, delaying working on the sales report you're expected to hand in by the end of the week is procrastinating, but putting off all other tasks you don't intend to do—say, go around the community helping Girl Scouts sell thin mints—isn't.

Unless, of course, helping the Girl Scouts sell 'em cookies is actually on your to-do list, and you deliberately put off doing it— then that's procrastination. You get the picture.

The defining feature of procrastination is that it involves putting off tasks you know are better off done now. It is essentially an act of avoiding discomfort (i.e. the trouble of doing the intended task) and pursuing pleasure instead (i.e. substituting more enjoyable activities, plus the relief of not having to engage in the intended task). Who needs help with pursuing pleasure, after all? That is rarely the problem that keeps us up at night.

Why do we procrastinate?

Since the time of ancient civilizations, our ancestors have struggled with the dilemma of choosing to do what needs to be done over other, usually more pleasant, activities. We may imagine that our less industrious forebears must have had days when they relaxed lying under a tree shade instead of picking up their spears to hunt or their baskets to forage for food. Hesiod, a Greek poet who lived around 800 B.C., cautioned not to "put your work off till tomorrow and the day after." Roman consul Cicero was also an early dissenter against procrastination, calling the act "hateful" in the conduct of affairs. This is clearly a problem that is older than we give it credit for.

So if procrastination has been around since time immemorial, where did the impulse for this habit come from? Has it been hardwired in our brains from the beginning?

Neurobiologists have found evidence that *yes*, the fundamental workings of our brains might indeed offer a recipe for procrastination. Remember that procrastination is the act of delaying an intended important task, despite knowing that there will be negative consequences as a result of it. In other words, we have no problem recognizing that procrastinating is likely to be bad for us. In fact, we rationally know it's something to avoid at all costs. What we do have a problem with is regulating ourselves enough to avoid that habit.

Our human logic knows procrastinating is bad, but our human impulses are often stronger and so automatic that willpower or awareness alone can't save us from indulging them.

Procrastination is thus essentially a failure of self-regulation. But why do we fail to regulate ourselves? Experts say it's because we're not that adept at keeping firm command over our capricious drives and impulses—and here's where neurobiologists lay out for the rest of us the biological basis of why we procrastinate.

Imagine the brain as having two major portions—one inner portion, and one outer portion. Now, at the inner portion is what some scientists call our "lizard brain," responsible for our most basic survival instincts. This region is fully developed from birth and controls our most primitive drives (e.g. hunger, thirst, and sex drive), as well as our mood and emotions (e.g. fear, anger, and pleasure). It's one of the most dominant portions of our brain, as its processes tend to be automatic, not to mention life-maintaining.

This portion is called the limbic system. It quite literally keeps us alive because we don't have to consciously think about breathing or becoming hungry; it just happens and we live to see another day.

The outer portion, enclosing the limbic system and situated just behind our forehead, is called the prefrontal cortex. While the limbic system has been dubbed as our "lizard brain," the prefrontal cortex has been identified by neurobiologists as the portion which separates us humans from lesser animals.

The prefrontal cortex is in charge of our rational human functions, such as assimilating information, planning, making decisions, and other higher-order thinking skills.

So while the limbic system just lets us experience instincts and emotions automatically, the prefrontal cortex requires us to put in conscious and deliberate effort to be able to think, plan, decide, and ultimately compete a task. The prefrontal cortex works much, much slower, and we are generally conscious of these thoughts.

By now, you may recognize how these two major portions of the brain must be continually engaged in battle, a battle which you feel most intensely when you're faced with something you would rather not do, but have to. In instances such as these, your limbic system is screaming, *"Don't do it! It doesn't feel good!"* while your prefrontal cortex is trying to reason with you, *"You have to do this."*

It's akin to what the well-known psychologist Sigmund Freud described as a constant battle between the instinctive, pleasure-driven id and the rational, reality-based ego. While the id cares only that you satisfy your impulses immediately, the ego has to consider the entire situation and the possible consequences of heeding the id's whims.

Thus, what experts are pointing to as the foundation of procrastination—the inability to manage drives and impulses—pertains to the inability of our prefrontal cortex to win over the whiny and spur-of-the-moment demands of our limbic system. The moment our prefrontal cortex lets up, we lose focus on a certain task and our limbic system is then quick to take the reins (remember, it's more automatic), moving us toward doing something more pleasurable instead.

Once we engage in that alternate activity, a brain chemical known as dopamine floods our brains. This is what creates the rush of pleasure we feel, and it's pretty addictive too. We are drawn to activities that stimulate actual dopamine release, as well as to those activities we perceive will likely lead to that dopamine rush.

In other words, what leads us to procrastinate is not just the *actual* pleasure from those activities, but more importantly, the pleasure we *expect* to feel in choosing those activities over another. This is the scientific explanation behind procrastination—we anticipate we're going to feel better doing something else, so we go ahead and do it.

Our expectation of feeling good if we procrastinate is what drives us to put off our intended tasks for the moment and engage in a different activity instead. This anticipation of pleasure is the mental equivalent of drooling over a sumptuous dish; it whets our appetite for biting into the shiny, yet poisoned fruit that is procrastination. Goodbye, homework; hello, old episodes of *I Love Lucy*.

For example, you arrive from your morning break at the office and find a pile of incoming correspondence on your desk. You know you should promptly review, sort, and distribute them as appropriate, but the thought of having to do it already fills you with boredom. Shopping online for what you're going to wear to your next office party—now that's exciting.

So you go online and start browsing party wear instead, and you're so filled with glee discovering new fashion finds that you quickly forget a pile of work is waiting for you. Your limbic system has successfully hoodwinked your prefrontal cortex with the lure of some dopamine candy, leading you to put off until tomorrow what you could and should have done today.

So if you've succumbed to procrastination like this too many times before, don't think that it's because you're a hopeless, lazy bum. Your limbic system might just be extra-cunning, or your prefrontal cortex just needs a little more tweaking and practice in taking control of the situation (or both). See, your prefrontal cortex is like a muscle that can be trained and exercised to get better at beating procrastination. You can teach it to run strategies that'll boost your willpower to help you start and stay on-task, jump past temptations, and hit the bull's-eye on your target goals.

As you can see, the underlying mechanism in procrastination is the lack of ability to regulate oneself, a task which the prefrontal cortex is in charge of. Noting this connection, researcher Laura Rabin of Brooklyn College wondered why, oddly enough, no one had ever examined the link between procrastination and the prefrontal cortex more closely.

To fill this gap in research, Rabin and her colleagues delved into a closer examination of the relationship between procrastination and major processes in the prefrontal cortex. These processes, which include planning, problem-solving, self-control, and the like, are collectively known as executive functioning.

Rabin's study assessed a sample of 212 students for procrastination, as well as the nine clinical subscales of executive functioning: (1) inhibition, (2) self-monitoring, (3) planning and organization, (4) activity shifting, (5) task initiation, (6) task monitoring, (7) emotional control, (8) working memory, and (9) general orderliness.

The researchers expected the first four of these subscales to be linked to procrastination. As it turned out, the results exceeded their expectations—all nine subscales were found to have significant associations with procrastination, as reported by Rabin and her colleagues in a 2011 issue of the *Journal of Clinical and Experimental Neuropsychology*.

Let's consider how each of these nine executive functions relates to procrastination.

Inhibition. This pertains to your ability to be "in control" of yourself, to resist impulses, and to stop your own behavior when it's appropriate to do so. Inability to perform this function well leads to impulsivity, which typically manifests as acting without thinking. If you're prone to acting without first considering the consequences of your actions, then you might have problems with inhibition.

Lack of inhibition is a key factor in procrastination. If you can't control yourself enough to resist the impulse of going for an easier, more pleasurable activity, then you'll always just be choosing to do virtually anything else other than what you're supposed to be doing. You'll always be giving in to the temptation to engage in a more enjoyable activity, rather than take the pains of sticking to your to-do list.

Say you've intended to spend your first hour at the office researching ideas for your marketing proposal. However, as you sit down to work on it, your phone keeps beeping with notifications from the lively social media scene. Lacking inhibitory control, you fail to resist checking your phone and engaging with your friends on social media, and thus you end up procrastinating on your intended research task.

Self-monitoring. This refers to your ability to monitor your own behavior and its effect on yourself and others. It involves a sense of social or interpersonal awareness, such that you not only recognize how you behave, but you also understand why people react the way they do toward you.

If impaired, you might have trouble perceiving both your progress and your delays, and you'll likely always be questioning why certain people treat you the way they do.

Impaired self-monitoring thus inevitably results in a severe lack of self-awareness. It means you can't think about your own thinking, and thus you can be ruled by your lizard brain without even being aware of it. When lacking such self-awareness and the ability to think about your thinking, you'll be more likely fall prey to destructive patterns of thought and bad habits, including procrastination.

Inadequate self-monitoring is thus linked with procrastination. When you're unaware of how you behave, you'll be less likely to even realize you're procrastinating. What's more, when you fail to recognize how your behavior impacts others, you'll be less likely to feel the pressure to deliver on your commitments, which means you'll feel freer to put off tasks to a later time.

Lack of self-monitoring will not only lead you to procrastinate, but also hinder you from taking steps to address it.

For instance, imagine you're set to update employee records one afternoon because an independent audit is coming up. However, instead of getting to the task, you get caught up in a conversation with your boss about the importance of keeping updated files. You feel there's nothing wrong with keeping the conversation going; after all, your discussion is relevant to the task. You fail to see that this very conversation is precluding you from actually doing the very task you're supposed to be doing. You're procrastinating, and you don't even realize it.

Planning and organization. This comprises your ability to manage present and future task demands. The planning component of this function is about your ability to set goals and map out the right order of steps to get the job done. The organization component pertains to your ability to pick up on the main ideas of a given information load and to bring order to information. Together, planning and organization involve your ability to anticipate future situations and demands accurately, and to take those into account as you lay out the steps necessary to achieve your goals.

Insufficient planning and organization is related to procrastination. If you lack the ability to set realistic goals and establish plans to meet those goals, you'll likely miss appreciating how much time you really have to accomplish your intended tasks. Thus, you'll feel at greater liberty to squander time procrastinating rather than getting to work.

Also, if you lack the skills to organize information, you'll likely fixate on irrelevant details of a task rather than work on the major stuff. The worst part about this is you won't feel like you're procrastinating because you'll think you're "working." In reality, though, you're avoiding the real job while working on extraneous little tasks to cover up your avoidance.

As an example, imagine you need to work on completing a financial report due two weeks from now. Lacking effective planning skills, you don't break down the task into smaller portions and don't set specific hours you're going to work on it. You simply go through the days doing whatever's pushed under your nose (fonts, formatting, and type of paper to print on) and relaxing when nothing's due on that day. You put off doing the report until you realize, much to your panic, that it's due in two hours' time.

Activity shifting. This reflects your ability to easily move from one activity to another, depending on the demands of the situation. If you're adept at activity shifting, you can make transitions effortlessly and tolerate change. This function also involves your ability to switch or alternate your attention as needed, and to shift your focus from one aspect of a problem to another. Consider this your ability to be flexible, in terms of both behavior and thinking.

A deficit in activity-shifting ability is linked with procrastination. After all, getting down to work basically constitutes a shift from non-working to working mode.

If you're unable to switch from rest mode or from one productive mode to another, then you'll end up procrastinating because you just can't get yourself to switch to the other side. You'll stagnate at your original state, either doing nothing or continuing an activity you're not supposed to be doing at the time.

Say you've been diligent enough to draw up a schedule for the day. You've written that you're going to do some gardening from 8:00 AM to 9:00 AM, then move inside the house and work on a manuscript from 9:00 AM to 11:00 AM. However, you're fully enjoying and so engrossed in your gardening that you continue with it well past the time you've set for it to stop.

You end up spending your entire morning just gardening because you lacked the ability to shift your focus and energy onto the next task as scheduled. This form of procrastination can be tricky to spot and address, as it can look like you're making good use of your time when in fact, you're not.

Task initiation. This pertains to your ability to simply start and get going on tasks or activities. It is what enables you to break the inertia of inactivity and take the first step on the task at hand—or on any task, for that matter. The first step is always the toughest to take.

Task initiation also includes your capacity to generate ideas and problem-solving strategies by yourself. If this function is weak, you'll find it very difficult to begin tasks or generate problem-solving approaches. It will feel like you can see a long, winding road stretching out before you, but you just can't lift your foot to take the first step and walk along it.

Problems in task initiation are related to procrastination. You find it difficult to start doing what you should be doing; instead, you continue engaging in other activities you find more enjoyable. You set a "start time" for each of your intended tasks, but once that moment arrives, you always find a reason to reschedule the start to another time.

Consider the following scenario: You need to prepare PowerPoint slides for a sales presentation. It's 8:30 AM. You say, "*I'll start at 9:00 AM*," and then you do other random, mindless things, supposedly to prep you for the busy day ahead. When you look back at the clock, you see it's 9:15 AM. So you figure, "*Nah, I'll start at 10:00 AM*." Sure, you may call it your "Perfectionist self just wanting to start things right," but you know what the real problem here is—you just can't find it in you to start.

Task monitoring. This refers to your ability to evaluate and keep track of your projects, as well as to identify and correct mistakes in your work. This also includes your ability to judge how easy or difficult a task will be for you and whether your problem-solving approaches are working or not. If your task monitoring function is impaired, you'll likely to find it difficult to weed out which tasks need to be done first, or you may forget what you need to do altogether.

Deficient task monitoring is associated with procrastination. If you lack the ability to track your tasks, you'll fail to prioritize your activities properly, leading you to focus on the less important stuff.

What's more, if you misjudge the difficulty of a certain task, you're more likely to put it off until later because you expect it to be easier than it actually is. A more realistic evaluation of the time and effort a task requires is essential to avoiding procrastination.

For instance, say you have a bunch of supply requests to review and approve. You estimate that it will take about an hour to finish all of them, and you've scheduled yourself to do the task during your last hour in the office. However, when that hour arrives, you don't feel motivated to proceed, so you put it off until tomorrow. After all, it will just take an hour.

Eventually, your attention is called as you've delayed the task for several days already and more work is piling up. When you finally sit down to work, you realize you've underestimated the time it takes to complete the task and regret all the time you wasted procrastinating.

Emotional control. This encompasses your ability to modulate or regulate your emotional responses. When your emotional control function is on point, you're able to react to events and situations appropriately. On the other hand, when your emotional control is problematic, you're likely to overreact to small problems, have sudden or frequent mood changes, get emotional easily, or have inappropriate outbursts.

Such inability to control your emotions is also likely to negatively impact your ability to control your thoughts. Emotions that run wild can derail the train of thought of even the most rational and intelligent people. So if you can't keep a lid on your emotions, you can't expect to be in full control of your thoughts—and your resulting actions—as well.

Problems with emotional control are related to procrastination. Remember the limbic system, that part of your brain that plays a significant role in your emotions, drives, and instincts? You're practically handing it the reins to direct your behavior if your prefrontal cortex lacks the ability to control your emotional responses.

Imagine how a baby behaves. Because it's not yet adept at emotional control, it mostly just responds to the whims of the limbic system (e.g., when it's hungry, it cries without regard for appropriateness of time and place). Likewise, if you're not adept at emotional control, you too will simply behave as you wish, aiming to reduce pain and increase pleasure at every moment.

Let's say you're trying to work out solutions for a financial problem at the company. This undertaking is important, but is causing you so much mental fatigue and distress that you decide to set it aside and pick up that entertaining phone of yours instead. The result? Procrastination.

Working memory. This comprises your capacity to hold information in your mind long enough to be able to complete a task. Your working memory is what enables you to follow complex instructions, manipulate information in your mind (e.g., do mental calculations), and carry out activities that have multiple steps.

If you've ever walked into a room and forgotten what you went there for, you've experienced a lapse in your working memory. Scientists and researchers routinely estimate average working memory at having a capacity of *seven, plus or minus two items.*

There's an apparent link between working memory and procrastination. See, working memory is what allows you to remember instructions and keep track of what you're doing. Problems in working memory can arise in two different ways. For some, working memory can be impaired by the presence of temptations and distractions in the environment, such as when an attractive ad pops up while you're doing serious research and it steals your attention away from your task.

For others, their working memory can simply be deficient, such as when they lose track of the information they're currently processing for seemingly no reason at all. For these people, their working memory just doesn't work, and so they're less likely to keep at tasks and more likely to procrastinate instead.

Either way, if your working memory is impaired, then you'll be prone to going off-task instead of keeping focused on what you need to do. You may have difficulty maintaining your attention on tasks that have multiple steps, leading you to stop halfway through and procrastinate instead.

Say you're tasked to review records of your project expenditures and prepare a progress report to inform upper management of your current project status. You had no problem getting yourself started on the task, but after looking over a couple of financial reports, you're finding it hard to keep track of the connections between the all the papers you've been reading. Unable to remain focused, you shift your attention to the office chatter happening at the next cubicle.

The next thing you know, you've joined your coworkers' conversation and have successfully abandoned your task for the day.

General orderliness. This refers to your ability to keep the things you need for projects well-organized and readily available, as well as to keep your workspaces orderly so that you're able to find whatever you need when you need it. General orderliness brings about efficiency in the way you work, as it allows you to spend less time looking for things and more time actually working on the task.

Lack of general orderliness is associated with procrastination. If your work area or living space is not well-organized, you'll be more likely to find yourself in situations when you need to get up from working and look for things, or even go out and buy materials you forgot you needed. You'll have veritable invitations for procrastination staring you in the face every moment of the day.

Distracted by these additional activities, you'll be more tempted to delay what you should be doing and instead engage in trivial activities. This applies even to the organization of files in your computer. If in your attempt to find one document, you need to sift through piles of folders with no discernable organizational scheme to them whatsoever, you're likely to come across other stuff that will distract you and lead you to procrastinate.

For instance, say you've sat down to create a module for a staff training session. After jotting down a few ideas, you realize you need to consult the company manual for certain considerations. So you get up to retrieve said manual, and on your way, you bump into another colleague, whom you end up chatting with over coffee at the pantry.

After losing about an hour to that, you manage to get back to your desk to try and work on the module again. You remember you have a computer file of an old module which you can use for reference, so you browse your folders looking for it. As you open folder after folder, you come across one bearing interesting articles you've saved for some light reading. You start reading one, then another, and another. Procrastination wins again.

In summary, procrastination may arise from problems in each of the nine executive functions—(1) inhibition, (2) self-monitoring, (3) planning and organization, (4) activity shifting, (5) task initiation, (6) task monitoring, (7) emotional control, (8) working memory, and (9) general orderliness.

Some people may have a habit of procrastinating because they have trouble stopping themselves from engaging in certain activities (inhibition), others may procrastinate because they find it challenging to start (task initiation), and so on. In other words, why and how you procrastinate may differ from the next person, because the executive function that underlies the problem may vary.

Can procrastination ever be useful?

Now, while the numerous ways procrastination can cause problems in your life have been well-covered, you may ask whether there's any value to procrastination at all, given it can be such an automatic tendency. Surely, nature can't be that bad at giving us a brain prone to procrastination when such habit doesn't offer any value at all.

Moreover, the fact that procrastinating has persisted as a habit of humans from ancient civilizations to the present time indicates there must be an evolutionary advantage to keeping that practice going. If procrastination has been around for this long, there must be times when there's good reason to pursue pleasure rather than delay gratification, right?

Right! It turns out there are at least five ways procrastination can actually be useful in certain instances.

First, there are times when certain tasks and obligations simply disappear of their own accord, so you won't need to complete your intended tasks after all. Evolutionary psychologist Dr. Doug Lisle explains that this was especially true in ancient times, when there was such uncertainty in the events that might transpire (e.g., people were more vulnerable to death by dismemberment and being eaten, etc.) that there was a good chance obligations and tasks would simply go away.

For instance, consider a hunter expected to provide food for a kinship of ten. If a portion of that kinship suddenly died because of a natural calamity, illness, or predation, then the hunter's task of providing for those who died would also go away. Thus, procrastinating in such an environment may have had value, as delaying work could've meant saving oneself from effort that would not have been necessary anyway.

In modern times, there's a lower likelihood that tasks and obligations will simply disappear, but it could still happen. For example, say you've been assigned to coordinate with a hotel manager to arrange for your company's gala in one of their function halls. You procrastinate on the task, failing to set up a meeting date and such.

A week later, you're informed that the gala venue has been changed and you won't need to coordinate with that hotel after all. In this case, your procrastination actually saved you the trouble of doing something that ended up being unneeded anyway.

Second, some types of procrastinating can push you to clear out the rest of your to-do list. This is because some tasks may seem so unpleasant to you that in order to avoid them, you would do anything, including the other tasks you need to do anyway.

Consider it this way: On your list of tasks, you typically have things that you actually look forward to doing, things you're okay doing, but not thrilled about, and things you really don't want to do. Given such gradation of the pleasantness or workability of tasks, you're bound to do whatever it takes to avoid that one task you find most abhorrent.

If you're what's called an "active procrastinator," you'll deal with this situation by taking up all the other tasks in your to-do list just to avoid having to do that one task you consider most objectionable.

The next thing you know, you've cleared the rest of your to-do list, leaving only that one task for you to now focus on because you've got no other choice. Here, procrastinating actually helped your procrastination problem.

To illustrate, imagine you're dreading having to do the liquidation report for your latest project. So instead of getting on with it, you check out the other tasks on your to-do list and systematically cross them off, one after another—you do research for your next project, write out a recommendations report for your boss, work out travel arrangements for your company trip, and so on. In this case, your procrastination on doing that liquidation report turns out to be beneficial, because it pushed you toward completing so many other tasks.

Third, procrastination can give you an opportunity to reevaluate tasks that may not be necessary or relevant. Putting off a task long enough can lead you to later look at it with fresh eyes and not even remember why it's on your to-do list. Recognizing it's unnecessary, you strike it off of your list. Procrastination has freed you from investing time and effort in something totally needless.

For example, say you've written out all the activities involved in making a resource management plan. You listed every single task, failing to see that some of those tasks (e.g., doing an inventory of current resources) fall under the responsibilities of another colleague. Fortunately, you've put off doing those tasks long enough to eventually realize (or be reminded!) that you should be delegating those things to a colleague instead of doing them yourself.

Fourth, procrastination may be a function of your intuition, working to help you avoid jumping into something that might not be right for you. This applies especially when it comes to procrastinating on making decisions. In such cases, your procrastination is usually born out of uncertainty as to which would be the best choice to make. It arises out of the conflicting voices of your rational mind and your gut feeling, providing you more time to really figure out which one to listen to.

By delaying the act of choosing, you get to first think through the pros and cons of each option and disentangle your own confusion about the situation. When the moment arrives that you no longer have a choice but to make a decision, you'll be better prepared to make the right one because you've done your research.

For instance, suppose you're trying to decide whether to stay at your current job or take a job offer at another company. While the new job offer is available for you to accept immediately, you delay deciding on it as you are unsure whether it's the best career move to make. In the meantime, you research both options and consider the pros and cons of each.

You discover that in a few months' time, you're up for a promotion in your current company, which would offer you better employment terms than if you take that other company's offer. So instead of jumping ship, you decide to stay.

In the above scenario, procrastinating on a decision turned out to be helpful to you, as it allowed you time to gather information and figure out the better option before committing to a decision. Had you made a choice right away, you likely would've jumped into something that wasn't the best option for you.

And fifth, procrastination may be your unconscious way of protecting yourself from the threat of failure. Fear of failure, according to Cal Newport, is what may underlie the compulsion to procrastinate. He explains that humans developed the ability for complex planning way before acquiring the capacity for verbal language.

So when you're about to get into a tricky situation in which you'll be prone to failing, it's unlikely there'll be a declaration in your head saying *"This plan's not gonna work!"* Instead, you'll experience a lack of motivation to start, likely resulting from a biochemical cascade released by your body to restrain you from going the wrong way.

Thus, you may imagine your brain standing at a crossroads, one leading you to work on the task and the other leading you to procrastinate. To decide where it will steer your body, your brain calculates the likelihood of you succeeding versus the possibility of you failing at your endeavor. The greater the risk of failure, the more likely your brain will push you toward the road to procrastinating. It understands that failure will not only feel disappointing, it will also bring about loss of status among your peers.

To protect your ego and save your self-esteem from being crushed by such failure and loss of status, your brain compels you to procrastinate. By putting off a task that's likely to fail anyway, you curb the possibility of having to survive the blow of failure and get to buoy your self-esteem.

As an example, imagine you're planning to develop a mobile game app. You've come up with a few rudimentary ideas about what the game will be. However, there are already a lot of more popular game apps very similar to it, and your idea really doesn't offer anything new to the market. You procrastinate on developing the app, but while you think it's just due to plain laziness, in reality it's because your mind is aware the app will likely be a flop. Instead of having you labor on something that will only fail in the future, your mind deprives you of the feeling of motivation to even start.

Thus, in certain circumstances, procrastination does have its merits. It may save you from exerting unnecessary effort, push you to clear other stuff in your to-do list more quickly, prevent you from engaging in irrelevant tasks, and steer you away from making rash decisions that are misguided and likely to lead you to failure. However, that procrastination is helpful rather than destructive is more the exception than the rule.

More often than not, procrastination can easily get out of hand and slowly eat away at your chances of achieving professional success and personal satisfaction. So how do you prevent procrastination from wreaking havoc in your life? Well, first things first: You've got to recognize the warning signs.

Takeaways:

- Procrastination has been around far longer than you or I. The term "procrastination" was derived from the Latin *pro*, meaning "forward, forth, or in favor of" and *crastinus*, meaning "of tomorrow." In everyday terms, it's when you put off something unpleasant, usually in pursuit of something more pleasurable or enjoyable.
- The pleasure principle is important to understand in the context of procrastination. Our brains have a constant civil war brewing inside; the impulsive and largely subconscious lizard brain wants immediate pleasure at the expense of the slower prefrontal cortex, which makes rational decisions. The prefrontal cortex makes the unpopular decisions which procrastination is not a fan of, while the lizard brain makes decisions that lead to

dopamine and adrenaline being produced. It may seem like a losing battle, but the key to battling procrastination is being able to regulate our impulses and drives—though not suppress them.

- It's been found that there are nine specific traits associated with procrastination. They include: (1) inhibition, (2) self-monitoring, (3) planning and organization, (4) activity shifting, (5) task initiation, (6) task monitoring, (7) emotional control, (8) working memory, and (9) general orderliness. Generally, deficiencies in any of these nine traits will make an individual more susceptible to procrastination. To beat procrastination, we must perform one of the hardest tasks of all: thinking about one's own thinking.

Chapter 2. Danger: Warning Signs

"You may delay, but time will not."
—Benjamin Franklin

Before you even attempt to rid your life of procrastination, you first need to be able to see *when* it's popping up in your life, *what* it looks like when it does, and *how* it is triggered. Not everyone procrastinates in the same way and for the same reasons, so knowing your personal tendencies and motivations is essential to later learning how to better handle yourself in the face of being tempted to procrastinate.

A doctor cannot effectively treat a patient without knowing what ails them, and similarly, we cannot handle our own brains without knowing what sets them into a frenzy of unproductivity.

Which type of procrastinator are you?

Drawing mostly from research by psychology professor Dr. Joseph Ferrari, Alina Vrabie identifies five types of procrastinators: (1) thrill-seeker, (2) avoider, (3) indecisive, (4) perfectionist, and (5) busy. Try to get a sense of what characterizes each type and figure out which one personifies you best. You might be a mixture of multiple types of procrastinators.

Thrill-seeker. Also known as the crisis-makers, thrill-seekers live for the last-minute rush. As the deadline looms nearer, they feel more pumped up and ready to work. Instead of feeling frazzled under the pressure of racing against the clock, thrill-seekers actually enjoy the sensation of working close to a deadline. Their procrastination is thus more intentional than accidental, as they're likely to be aware of the boost in energy they feel as things get right down to the wire. If they're procrastinating, it's because they intend to. These are the people who claim to be able to work best under the stress of a deadline.

Obviously very confident in their capacity to produce quality output even with limited time, thrill-seekers feel that they work best under pressure and crave the adrenaline rush that comes with the experience. They deliberately leave the work untouched until the last minute so they can get that dose of adrenaline and thrill that they seek. This is part of what psychologist Mark Zuckerman calls "sensation-seeking," a trait more dominant in some people than in others.

For example, Lawrence is assigned to prepare a presentation that will introduce the company's new product in an upcoming launch. He has a month to work on it and make it an informative and engaging presentation. However, for weeks, he feels no motivation to start preparing the presentation. It was only a day before the scheduled launch that he felt a rush of creative ideas and energy to finally begin putting together the presentation. Lawrence is a classic thrill-seeker, procrastinating when there's plenty of time left and then feeling the rush to complete the task only moments before the deadline.

Avoider. Avoiders put off tasks until a later time in order to avoid being judged based on their output. While you may think that avoiders steer away from work because they find the tasks boring or tiring, in actuality, what avoiders are trying to run away from is the threat of failure, or in some instances, even that of success.

They are typically self-conscious and highly concerned with what other people might think. Especially when given high-stakes tasks, avoiders shrivel up in fear of either messing up the entire thing or discovering what they're truly capable of.

Now, the avoiders' fear of failure is easy enough to understand—failure often causes people to lose confidence, credibility, and status. But fear of success? Why would avoiders be afraid of finding out their strengths and succeeding at their tasks?

The avoiders' fear of success is rooted in a sense of having to feel guilt and responsibility once they do discover the fullest extent of their capacities. If they work on a task and accomplish it with flying colors, they're likely to feel guilt for all the other times they performed below their potential. In addition, they're also likely to feel a staggering responsibility to continue performing at their fullest capacities for the rest of the tasks they'll encounter in the future.

This is an awful lot of uncomfortable feelings and thoughts to carry about unconsciously, so their psyches attempt to save them from the discomfort by compelling them to procrastinate instead.

That way, they're saved from the guilt and responsibility of recognizing their fullest potentials.

Say Nicole is an avoider who's tasked to come up with a charity project for her organization. She has a lot of ideas as to how to go about the project, but she acts on none of them for fear that they won't work out. Thus, instead of getting going on the task, she immerses herself in other activities, some of which are projects unrelated to what she's assigned to do while others are recreational activities— anything to avoid having to work on a task she fears she's going to fail at.

Indecisive. Indecisives procrastinate because they don't want to be held responsible for a negative outcome. Unlike avoiders who fear either failure or success, indecisives mainly fear blame. While avoiders procrastinate to evade the judgment that comes *after* completing a task, indecisives procrastinate in order to shift the responsibility of doing the task at the *present* moment.

They attempt to put off having to make a decision or start on a task in the hopes that if they delay long enough, someone else will make the decision in their stead, or the task might somehow be removed from their workload. If they weren't the ones who made the decision, then they couldn't be blamed if the decision turned out to be a mistake. If they never got to work on a task, then they couldn't be blamed for a negative outcome.

Their fear of blame far exceeds their desire for recognition, so they prefer not to take the risk of deciding or working on a task at all.

Take, for instance, Mike, an indecisive procrastinator. He's been put in-charge of an ad hoc committee tasked with developing a training program for company interns. His supervisor has asked him to submit a draft of the program three times now, but he still hasn't complied. He's delaying making the final call on important aspects of the program because he's afraid he might get blamed if it turns out to be a flop.

Perfectionist. Perfectionists delay tasks for fear that they're going to do things wrong. They've set standards for themselves and don't settle for a "job well done" or even "excellent job"; rather, they want nothing less than utter perfection. Now, you might wonder: If they want to achieve perfection, aren't they supposed to be the ones working super-hard in an attempt to perfect their work, instead of lying about doing nothing or engaging in irrelevant activities?

Well, no. Perfectionists have set such high standards that the thought of attempting to measure up to those yardsticks fills them with paralyzing dread. As long as they don't touch a task, it still has the potential to be perfect. But once they start on the task, there's now a very real possibility of messing it up, with some errors potentially causing irreversible damage.

They're not necessarily as concerned with other people's opinions as avoiders are, nor do they have a fear of making decisions as indecisives do, but perfectionists tend to hold significantly higher standards than avoiders and indecisives do.

To escape the pressure of having to meet those sky-high standards, perfectionists simply leave tasks untouched and prefer instead to procrastinate. You would be right to also think that perfectionists are often people deathly afraid of judgment, just in disguise.

Say Sheena is tasked with updating the company manual with newly approved policies and procedures. Although completely capable of handling the job, she resists touching the manual for weeks for fear that she might deliver a less-than-perfect job. After all, the entire company is going to use the manual, so it needs to be flawless. Afraid of making mistakes, Sheena thus engages in other activities that will distract her from working on the manual, from reorganizing her office workspace to color-coding the file folders.

Busy. Busy procrastinators want to do it all, all at once. In their attempt to cover everything, they fail to actually get anything done. Their to-do list is crammed with tasks that all appear equally important to them. Thus, they typically start on one task, feel overwhelmed by the seeming urgency of another, jump to that other task, and then again think of another task they *really* have to get started on, jump on a different task again, and so on.

Busy procrastinators appear to be perpetually in motion, but strangely never get to tick any single task off their to-do list. The main ability they lack is prioritizing, which leaves them fussing over too many tasks instead of working on them systematically. In reality, they're constantly in motion, but not necessarily working toward anything major.

For example, Chris is an energetic manager who always has a long list of things-to-do, from following up with individual team members to writing reports and organizing capacity-building seminars. He always seems to be on the go, but somehow is still often late for meetings and never gets to submit paperwork on time. Chris personifies the busy procrastinator: always working, but never done.

What triggers you to procrastinate?

Each of the different types of procrastinators—thrill-seeker, avoider, indecisive, perfectionist, and busy—tends to have a different trigger for procrastinating. Some are greatly influenced by external activities and triggers in the environment, while others are more affected by internal mental and emotional factors.

Thrill-seekers are triggered by any activity around them that's irrelevant and enjoyable enough to allow them to push back their intended task to the last minute. Busy procrastinators are also triggered to put off tasks through actions that allow them to start as many things as possible, but not finish any of them. Thrill-seekers and busy procrastinators are thus both largely influenced by action-based triggers—activities and prompts in their immediate environments that breed procrastination.

On the other hand, avoiders are prompted by the emotion of fear of either failure or success. Indecisives are triggered also by fear, but this time, that of blame. Perfectionists are pressured by their own mental models of what they consider worthy work (i.e., only perfection).

Thus, what leads avoiders, indecisives, and perfectionists to procrastinate are mental/emotion-based triggers that drain them of the energy and motivation to work on their intended tasks. What's more, once they're considerably fatigued and stressed, their willpower to fight against procrastinating further declines, leading to a downward spiral of their chances of ever completing their tasks.

So as you see, there are two general kinds of triggers for procrastinating: action-based and mental/emotion-based.

First, action-based triggers are environmental prompts and physical activities that support the continued practice of procrastination. For example, you may start clearing your desk to make space for the work you intend to do, but end up wiping it down with disinfectant, organizing the papers you found lying about, and eventually cleaning and organizing the rest of your office.

Remember that while sticking to a task requires conscious effort, procrastination is more automatic. Thus, when there are prompts all around you which trigger you to act on that automatic impulse, then you'll end up simply delaying what you need to do in order to indulge those triggers.

Action-based triggers involve what you find yourself doing when you start to procrastinate. For instance, you decide to go on social media for a quick breather from your task. What you planned to be a five-minute check on your notifications evolves into a two-hour-long break, scrolling on your feed and chatting with your friends.

Another example is when you start your morning by drafting a schedule of what you intend to do for the day, then find yourself drawing up a schedule for tomorrow, and the rest of the week, the entire month, and so on.

You might end up with your five-year career plan by the end of the day, but discover you haven't even accomplished item number one on your to-do list.

Thus, it is important to be aware of these action-based triggers, catch yourself once you start to do them, and know how to deal with them appropriately to get yourself back on track. Try to look back on your habits and notice the patterns of procrastination you may fall into. Being aware of your go-to activities once you get bored or find the task too difficult is the key to catching yourself procrastinating next time.

For example, you may notice that once you lose interest or focus on a task, you automatically open up your browser and start entertaining yourself with YouTube videos. Knowing this tendency, you will later be more adept at catching yourself procrastinating, and thus address it promptly or put in place strategies to make it harder for you to fall into its trap the next time.

The second kind of trigger for procrastinating involves your mental and emotional states. As mentioned, irrational thoughts (e.g., impossibly high expectations) and uncomfortable emotions (e.g. fear) may already be working to undermine your motivation to work. Add to that triggers such as physical fatigue, lack of sleep and exercise, unhealthy diet, and feelings of isolation from lack of social support, and you'll surely have lower resistance against procrastination.

For instance, say you're an avoider whose fear of failure is already taking up much of your mental energy to deal with. You're tasked to design a company logo for a client, but you delay working on it because you're unsure of your ability to deliver quality output. Over the week, you're also exhausted from your active avoidance of the task, as you took on numerous other less important ones which left you feeling mentally and physically drained.

Feeling like you're in no condition to get the creative juices flowing, you feel even more compelled to put off the task until a later time. Had you taken better care of yourself and saved your energy for your intended task, you would've been in a better condition to feel motivated to do it.

Are you just impulsive?

In getting to know the warning signs of procrastination, one of the main things you should consider is impulsivity.

Impulsivity means acting immediately on an impulse, whether it be a passing thought, a sudden emotion, or an instantaneous desire. Consider the common procrastination habits you may have. When you're bored with a task, it may occur to you how nice it would be to grab a bite first and relax watching an episode of your favorite sitcom, and the next second, you've abandoned your work and plopped down in front of the TV with a bag of chips.

Procrastination may have many other ways of manifesting other than that, but its many faces all have one thing in common: They arise out of an impulsive tendency to do what feels easier or more enjoyable, rather than stick it out doing what you need to do until it's done. Why does this tend to happen, and why is this impulsive tendency so hard to fight? Are you just an impulsive person with low self-control?

The answer is in your brain's natural working mechanisms. If you may recall, there's a constant battle between your limbic system's strong desire to seek pleasure and avoid pain, and your prefrontal cortex's rational planning and decision-making controls. But while the prefrontal cortex's tasks require conscious effort to carry out, the limbic system's impulses are primitive and automatic.

Unless your prefrontal cortex has been training for years and earned a black belt in limbic system control, it's likely to lose the fight against the more compelling and instinctive impulses of the limbic system.

Thus, though you may be fully aware that you'd really be better off doing the task now rather than putting it off until tomorrow (prefrontal cortex's move), you would still be more likely to be swayed into engaging in easier, more pleasurable tasks in the immediate moment (limbic system's countermove). This is the neurobiological mechanism underlying the impulsivity common among procrastinators.

Impulsivity is characterized by four broad characteristics, as detailed by behavioral researchers Martial Van der Linden and Mathieu d'Acremont in a 2005 study published in *The Journal of Nervous and Mental Disease*.

First, impulsivity involves urgency. You feel that you need to be in a rush to do something right this moment. For instance, you may feel compelled to check your social media accounts right now, and delaying it only fills you with mounting tension.

Second, there's lack of premeditation. You act without thinking or planning your actions, often with a relative disregard toward how such actions will affect you in the future. For example, even though you've just taken a break, you agree to a colleague's spontaneous invitation to another coffee break because you're finding your current task to be too monotonous. You fail to appreciate how unnecessarily taking yet another 15 minutes off-task is bound to affect the progress, timeliness, and quality of your work.

Third, there's lack of perseverance. You easily lose motivation and are prone to giving up on tasks that require prolonged effort. For instance, instead of staying at your desk long enough to finish the inventory report you're supposed to accomplish before lunch, you lose steam halfway through and spend the rest of the morning chatting with your workmates.

And fourth, impulsivity is characterized by sensation-seeking. You crave that feel-good sensation that comes from engaging in activities that you find thrilling, enjoyable, or exciting. For example, you can't sit still and endure the monotony of typing out data on a computer because you're itching to go online and experience the thrill of playing World of Warcraft again.

Now, add those four characteristics together—urgency, lack of premeditation, lack of perseverance, and sensation-seeking—and what you get is a person who's quickly derailed from working on their intended task and instead follows their spur-of-the-moment desires. The stronger these four tendencies are in yourself, the more likely you'll set aside what you need to do in order to go for what feels good at the moment.

It doesn't matter that you've planned to do a task for weeks. The only thing that matters to you, at that very instant, is that you get to do what you feel like doing. Your new impulse feels just as urgent to you as the intended task you've known about for weeks.

Impulsivity is a key feature of a number of mental disorders, such as attention-deficit/hyperactivity disorder (ADHD) and substance abuse. People with ADHD may engage in hasty actions or decisions without first thinking of their possible consequences. For example, they may agree to do a job without knowing enough information about it, use other people's things without asking permission, or intrude into conversations by cutting others off mid-sentence.

They do these things not because they want to make a fool of themselves or intend to be rude, but because they lack the ability to stop themselves from acting on their immediate impulses.

If you believe you have the tendency to be impulsive, there are certain things you can do to curb that inclination. One strategy is to use the HALT method, a popular strategy originally taught in addiction recovery programs.

Before acting or making a decision, first be conscious of any feeling of Hunger, Anger, Loneliness, or Tiredness you may have. If you're feeling any of these, you're more likely to make rash, misguided decisions and act on your impulses that may lead you right into trouble. Thus, before jumping into anything, first consider the HALT factors and address any of them which may be weakening your resolve or influencing your decision-making.

Suppose you just came out of a meeting and you're angry at one of your colleagues because he threw you under the bus for a grave error on a project you both collaborated on. You go back to your desk and try to finish another report that's due within the hour, but you feel the urge to abandon it altogether. Before you do, recognize that your impulse to procrastinate might just be triggered by your anger.

Understanding this link, you can then consider how delaying the report will only further hurt your performance standing as an employee—which, given recent events, you cannot afford to let happen. So before jumping into any rash actions, recognize that the anger pushing you to procrastinate would not be the best thing to allow at this time. You may need to calm yourself first and change your perspective of the situation in order to regain control of yourself and not give in to procrastination.

Another strategy to help you be less impulsive is to recall the benefits of delaying gratification and perform a cost-benefit analysis for waiting. Before doing this, remember that you need to clear the HALT factors first so that your ability to consider the benefits of waiting won't be compromised. No one would want to wait any longer if they were hungry, angry, lonely or tired. Once you've established that you're free of HALT, consider how waiting at present would benefit you in the future.

For instance, imagine you're torn between completing a marketing plan summary at the office and bolting from work for three hours to catch a movie with your friends. While the prospect of relaxing in front of the big screen while sharing popcorn with your hilarious friends is definitely enticing, first recall the benefits of resisting that temptation and sticking with your task instead.

If you stay, you'll avoid getting into trouble at work, be able to cross off a major task from your to-do list, and get to fully enjoy the movie later instead of having to watch it while worried sick you might incur the wrath of your boss. Thus, delaying gratification appears to be the better option.

In conclusion, a number of warning signs can indicate a looming bout of procrastination. Depending on the type of procrastinator you are (thrill-seeker, avoider, indecisive, perfectionist, or busy), you may be triggered to procrastinate by certain actions, mental states, emotions, or even physical stress and fatigue. Impulsivity is also a key tendency that can derail you from focusing on what you should be doing and lead you to indulging in whatever feels good at the moment. To address these warning signs, you'll first need to have enough self-knowledge to be aware when they're affecting you. Upon recognizing the signs, you can then utilize strategies that'll help you win against procrastination, starting with developing a better mindset.

Takeaways:

- This chapter is about the warning signs that procrastination is imminent. There are far too many to name, but there are a few common types that can be helpful to articulate and then diagnose in yourself. They come in the context that there are generally five different types of procrastinators: (1) thrill-seeker, (2) avoider, (3) indecisive, (4) perfectionist, and (5) busy. Each type has its own triggers, like the feeling of adrenaline and risk, avoiding rejection, and feeling overwhelmed. They can generally be grouped into two general kinds of procrastination triggers: action-based and mental/emotion-based.

- No matter the warning signs for you, they might not matter if you are simply an impulsive person who disregards rational thought and lives in the moment. This might sound positive, but it is not a pretty sight. Four traits make up impulsivity: urgency (I must do this right now), lack of premeditation (I don't know how this will affect me later), lack of perseverance (I'm tired of this, what else is there to do?), and sensation-seeking (Oh, that feels better than what I am currently doing). The more elevated your levels, the more impulsive and procrastinating you will be.

- A helpful method for defeating procrastination is called HALT, and it stands for Hunger, Anger, Loneliness, or Tiredness. When you are facing a fork in the road in regards to persevering or procrastinating, ask yourself if any of the HALT factors are present. If any are, understand that you are already predisposed to making a poor decision and try to regulate your thoughts.

Chapter 3: Anti-Procrastination Mindsets

"If and When were planted, and Nothing grew."
—Proverb

As discussed in the previous chapters, procrastination is mainly the result of the prefrontal cortex lacking control over the limbic system's stronger and more automatic impulses. Thus, to counter procrastination, you'll need to train your prefrontal cortex to get better at exerting control over the whims of the limbic system. This process entails building anti-procrastination mindsets—outlooks and approaches that get you off your butt to deal with the options you come across with in more productive ways.

There are at least three ways you can build a mindset that's iron-clad against the ever-constant lure of procrastination: (1) mastering the physics of productivity, (2) eliminating the paradox of choice, and (3) finding the right motivation to kick-start action.

Master the Physics of Productivity

Who would have thought that productivity and procrastination could be viewed through the lens of physics, math, and equations? James Clear found a way to do so using Newton's Three Laws of Motion as an analogy to formulate the Three Laws of Productivity.

By getting to dissect procrastination as physics concepts and equations with identifiable elements and interactions, you'll get to identify the specific things you need to do or to avoid in order to add to your productivity and subtract from your procrastination. If you know the variables at work when you procrastinate, then you'll literally be able to single out a particular variable and manipulate it, as you're able to do in a mathematical equation.

The three laws of motion were formulated by physicist Sir Isaac Newton in 1687 to explain how physical objects and systems move and are affected by the forces around them. He's the guy who claims to have conceived of gravity after getting hit by a falling apple.

These laws lay the foundation for understanding how things from the smallest machine parts to the largest spacecraft and planets move. And now applied to the science of human cognition and behavior, these laws can also illuminate the mechanisms behind procrastination—and how to manipulate those mechanisms to drive productivity instead.

First law of motion. According to Newton's first law of motion, an object at rest tends to remain at rest, and an object in motion continues to be in motion unless an outside force acts upon it. How this law applies to the phenomenon of procrastination is glaringly evident: An object at rest tends to remain at rest, which means a person in a state of rest tends to remain at rest—unless some sort of force moves him or her into action.

So if you're currently in a state of inaction with regard to your intended task, you'll tend to remain inactive unless you're stimulated into motion. Your tendency to leave that task untouched is thus a fundamental law of the universe.

But before you start to think being a perpetual procrastinator is therefore a hopeless case, remember that Newton's first law of motion works the other way too: An object in motion continues to be in motion, which means a person in a state of action tends to continue moving as well. So if you're currently working on a task, this law of motion states that you'll tend to keep working on that task.

So what does this mean in the context of productivity and procrastination? The most critical element of beating procrastination is to find a way to start. Find a way to get moving. Once you get the ball rolling, it gets infinitely easier to keep going until the task is done.

Now, the next question becomes: How do you get started on a task? James Clear suggests following what's known as the Two-Minute Rule as applied to productivity. The rule states that you need to start your task in less than two minutes from the time you start thinking about it. Think of it as a personal contract you strike with yourself. No matter what, you need to start within the next two minutes.

For example, suppose you're tasked to write a report detailing your department's project updates. To beat the inertia of lazing around the entire morning, commit to just jotting down the project title and objectives or expected output within the next two minutes. You don't need to think about doing the rest of it just yet. You need only start within the next two minutes. This action will help break the inactivity that's been strapping you down, and once you've started writing things down about your project, you'll find it easier to keep going.

Another benefit of abiding by this rule is that you'll also be forced to break the task down into smaller and smaller steps, as giving yourself a two-minute limit for starting requires you to think in terms of more manageable chunks of work you can start quick and easy.

Note that the Two-Minute Rule doesn't require you to pledge that you finish your task, or even to proceed with your task in an orderly manner. It doesn't need you to mind the quality of your output just yet; you can reserve the critiquing and refining of it for later. It just needs you to start, to get into motion.

This relieves a lot of the pressure that typically paralyzes you from touching a task and thus leads you down a path of procrastination. With Newton's first law of motion, you'll find that once you start, you will tend to keep going on your task. So rather than wait for an enormous amount of motivation before starting, just go ahead and start small.

You'll find that your motivation will snowball into ever-larger amounts after you've started.

Second law of motion. Newton's second law of motion explains how a particular force affects the rate at which an object is moving. It is represented by the equation $F=ma$, which states that the sum of forces (F) acting on an object is the product of that object's mass (m, which refers to how much matter there is in an object) and its acceleration (*a*, which is the rate of change in how fast an object is going).

In other words, the second law of motion dictates how much force is needed in order to accelerate an object of a particular mass toward a certain direction. And as illustrated by the equation, the relationship between these three variables—force, mass, and acceleration—is proportional.

The greater the mass of an object, the greater the force required to accelerate it. Likewise, the faster you need an object to move over time (i.e., accelerate), the greater the force you'll need to apply.

So if you want to accelerate an object—say, a ball—then the amount of force you exert on that ball, as well as the direction of that force you apply on the ball, will both make a difference. If more force is applied for the ball to go left than for it to go right, then you can bet that ball will go left.

Still with me?

Applied to productivity, this means that you'll need to pay attention not only to the amount of work you're doing (magnitude), but also to where you're applying that work (direction). If you work a lot, but don't focus all that work in a single direction, then you'll tend to accomplish less than when you direct the same amount of work to only one direction.

The amount of work you're able to do as a person has its limits, so if you want to make the most out of your effort, you need to start being conscious of where that work goes. As Newton's $F=ma$ equation teaches, where you direct your effort is just as important as how much effort you exert. Temptations, distractions, and lack of task prioritization all serve to scatter your energy and effort in different directions, so avoiding them is key to optimizing your productivity.

Say you have a myriad of things to accomplish before the day is up—reply to five client emails, read and critique a lengthy research plan, and write a recommendation letter for a former employee.

Applying Newton's second law, you need to recognize that how fast you'll be able to accomplish a particular task depends largely on your ability to focus the effort you exert on that task and that task only. If you insist on scattering the "force" you exert by frequently switching tabs from email to research to letter-writing all throughout the morning, you'll be less likely to accomplish any one of them before the lunch hour. You may even just be switching back and forth on those tasks as a way to procrastinate on all of them.

To remedy this, apply the principle of Newton's second law: Exert your force toward a single direction for its maximum acceleration.

Third law of motion. This law of motion states that "For every action, there is an equal and opposite reaction." This means that when Object A applies a force on Object B, Object B simultaneously applies a force of the same amount, but of opposite direction, on Object A. For example, when you swim, you apply force on the water as you push it backward. Simultaneously, the water applies a force on you that's equal in magnitude, yet opposite in direction, thus pushing you forward.

Applied to the science of productivity and procrastination, this law reflects how in your own life there are often productive and unproductive forces at work as well. There is a constant battle, and everyone's level of balance is different. For those who are unproductive, their unproductive forces tend to win more often than not.

Productive forces include positivity, atmosphere, environment, social network, focus, and motivation, while unproductive forces include stress, temptation and distraction, unrealistic work goals, and unhealthy lifestyles (e.g., poor diet or lack of sleep). The interaction and balance between these opposite forces is what creates your typical levels of productivity, as well as your usual patterns of procrastination.

This balance could shift either way—it could lead you to be massively productive, or to severely procrastinate. For example, it may take you just an hour to finish writing a report when you're feeling well-rested and confident in your abilities, but need a week to complete the same task when you're feeling stressed out and insecure.

Basing on the applications of Newton's third law of motion, there are two ways you can go about to up your productivity level and avoid procrastination. The first is to add more productive forces.

This is what James Clear refers to as the "power through it" option, in which you simply find a way to pump yourself up with more energy in an attempt to overpower the unproductive forces inhibiting you from working. This strategy may involve such actions as chugging cup after cup of coffee and digesting motivational words through books or inspirational videos.

The "power through it" option could work well, but only for a brief time. The problem with this strategy is that you're only trying to cover up the unproductive forces that are still working to undermine your productivity, and this tiring task could easily lead to burnout.

As an alternative, Clear suggests dealing with unproductive forces directly through the second option, which is to subtract, if not totally eliminate, unproductive forces. This strategy involves such actions as reducing the number of tasks you commit to, learning how to say no, and changing your environment in order to simplify your life.

Compared to the first option, which requires you to add more productive forces, this second option simply needs you to release the reservoir of energy and productivity already within you by removing the barriers that obstruct it. As you can imagine, this second option is an easier way to defeat procrastination than to have to produce productivity by attempting to add more productive forces.

For example, say you need to accomplish a year-end evaluation report for your organization's project sponsor. You're aware that you're the type of worker who needs quiet in order to think and work effectively, but your office cubicle is between two chatty colleagues. Instead of simply opting to "power through" the task despite the noisy and distracting environment you're in (i.e., attempting to increase your productive forces), consider relocating to a quieter area or politely asking your colleagues to refrain from disturbing you for the next hour or two (i.e., eliminating unproductive forces).

That way, you'll be more motivated to start and keep working on a task, not necessarily because you've upped your willpower, but because you've simply let the natural energy already within you flow unhindered.

Eliminate the Paradox of Choice

While most people tend to think having choices is good—and the more choices there are, the better—current research on human behavior actually suggests otherwise. In a phenomenon that psychologist Barry Schwartz calls the paradox of choice, people tend to be worse off when they have more options to choose from as opposed to when they have a single course of action available to them.

For example, suppose your company offers multiple types of research grants you can apply for. Pressured to make the "best" choice among all your options, and overwhelmed by the details and comparisons you need to sift through to be able to do so, you put the whole research thing on the back burner and leave it untouched for years. With zero additional research studies under your belt, you suffer career stagnation simply because in the face of multiple options, you've been too paralyzed to do anything.

Learning how to deal with the paradox of choice is thus a necessary technique to beat procrastination. If you've established a mindset that's able to promptly make sound decisions in the face of multiple options, then you'll less likely fall into the paralysis or stress that causes most people to procrastinate.

The paradox of choice tends to impact things negatively because once people become overwhelmed with too many options, one of two things tend to happen.

One, after making a choice, you may still constantly think about the other options that you didn't choose. For instance, after buying a painting, you may still fixate on imagining how great the other paintings you didn't buy would look in place of the one you bought. So you're never really satisfied with the choices you make, because a part of you remains preoccupied with thoughts of all the other options you missed out on by making a choice. It is the ultimate case of buyer's remorse.

Two, having too many options can subject you to a very difficult time deciding, such that you become paralyzed from making a decision and from doing anything at all. In philosophy, this is illustrated by the paradox of Buridan's ass (quite literally, donkey).

Popularized by philosopher Jean Buridan, this paradox tells of a hungry donkey standing between two identical piles of hay. The donkey always chooses the hay closer to him, but this time both piles are of equal distance from him. Unable to choose between the two piles, the donkey starves to death.

Applied to the mechanisms of work and productivity, the paradox of choice thus ultimately leads you to procrastinate, as you delay making a decision or starting on a task in an attempt to avoid the overwhelming pressure you feel from having so many options. The availability of options creates the illusion of greater personal responsibility to make not only the right choice, but the best one.

To beat the paradox of choice, the key is to set rules and restraints upon yourself. You'll need to find a way to see things in black-and-white, because gray areas are fertile grounds that breed overthinking and procrastination.

That spectrum of gray is likely to see you get stuck and agonize over which shade of gray is the best choice, until you get tired of the uncertainty, lose motivation, and end up being paralyzed from making any choice and acting at all. When Buridan's donkey saw shades of gray instead of one defined path to one defined dish of food, he faltered and ultimately starved to death.

To avoid falling into that trap, use the following strategies.

Focus on one factor and willfully ignore everything else. Every option is sure to offer its own pros and cons, and deciding among numerous options is not merely a matter of tabulating which has the most pros and the least cons. Rather, making a choice depends heavily on what you really care about, which often boils down to only one or two critical factors.

So instead of having to deal with countless criteria that can overwhelm you from making a choice, focus only on one or two vital factors and ignore the rest. That way, you have a clearer idea about which option is best for you, and you can select it faster too.

Suppose you need to buy a new microwave and have multiple models lined up in front of you, each with its own set of features and unique innovations. If you don't know which factors you want to focus on, it's easy to get confused by all the bells and whistles that such a large selection offers.

So to make it easier for you to make a choice that's really suited to your needs, decide beforehand on one or two specific features you want to mainly base your choice on—say, size (i.e., must fit your kitchen space) and sensor cooking. With just these two features in mind, you get to eliminate a lot of other models that don't fit the bill, thus effectively narrowing down your choices to make it easier for you to select the right one.

Set a time limit on making a decision. Commit to making a decision within, say, two minutes, tops. Whatever decision you arrive at by the end of two minutes, stick with it no matter what. This defeats the paradox of choice by putting a cap on the amount of time you spend agonizing over which decision to make. It saves you from suffering the negative consequences of letting things pass you by and spurs you into the action necessary to realize your goals.

For example, imagine you're in charge of choosing and facilitating the venue for your upcoming gala, but you're torn between Venue A and Venue B. You've put off making reservations for weeks now, simply because you can't decide which venue would be the better choice. To save yourself from wasting any more time procrastinating, set two minutes for you to come up with a decision and pledge to stick with it.

You may go back and forth between the two venues within those two minutes, but once the time is up, whatever venue you settle on should be the one you go for—say, Venue A. To strengthen this strategy (no backsies!), make sure to call and make reservations for Venue A by the end of the two minutes.

Immediately choose a default option and stick with it if no better alternative comes up. Once you've selected one option as the default, you can set a short amount of time to try to find alternatives and weigh them against your default choice. If none of the alternatives measure up to your default, then you just revert to that default choice. That way, you're ensured of having already made a decision beforehand, which you can simply follow through with once it's time to act.

The fact that you've chosen a default already constitutes a choice in itself, one which you'll most likely be inclined to stick with and follow through.

For example, again imagine you're in charge of choosing the venue for your upcoming gala, but you're so torn between Venue A and Venue B that you've put off facilitating the task altogether.

To save yourself from further procrastinating, you may set Venue A as your default choice, then allow three days for you to continue searching for other alternatives or to continue comparing the pros and cons between Venue A and Venue B. If by the end of the third day you find yourself either unconvinced by the other options, or so convinced by all of them you're now confused, then just revert to your default choice of Venue A.

That way, you can start moving on with the rest of your event planning instead of getting stuck and procrastinating because you can't make a choice. Training your mind to select a default option preps it to be more inclined toward active decision-making, rather than toward the passivity and paralysis that breeds procrastination habits.

Finally, strive to satisfice your desires more often than not. The word *satisfice* is a combination of the words *satisfy* and *suffice*. It's a term that Herbert Simon coined in the 1950s, and it represents what we should shoot for rather than something that is guaranteed to optimize and maximize our happiness.

Generally, people can be split into those two categories: those who seek to satisfice a decision and those who seek to maximize a decision.

Let's suppose that you are shopping for a new bike. The maximizer would devote hours to researching their decision and evaluating as many options as possible. They would want to get the best one possible for their purposes and want to leave no stone unturned. They want 100% satisfaction, despite the law of diminishing returns and the Pareto principle, which would warn against such measures.

By contrast, the satisficer is just shooting to be satisfied and is looking for an option that suffices for their purposes. They want something that works well enough to make them satisfied and pleased, but not overjoyed or ecstatic. They aim for *good enough* and stop once they find that.

These are very different scales, and for this reason, studies have shown that satisficers tend to be happier with their decisions while maximizers tend to keep agonizing and thinking about greener pastures after their decisions.

Maximization represents a conundrum in our modern age, because while it is more possible now than at any other point in human history to get exactly what you want, there is also the paradox of choice, which makes it impossible to be satisfied. On a practical matter, there are few decisions where we should strive to maximize our value. Therefore, put forth proportional effort and just make a choice already.

Most of the time, you simply want something that is reliable and works. Suppose you are in a grocery store and you are trying to pick out the type of peanut butter you want. What should you shoot for here? Satisficing or maximizing? The same type of thinking should apply to 99% of our daily decisions.

Otherwise, we are constantly overwhelmed and waste our mental bandwidth where there are diminishing returns. Whatever net benefit the most optimal type of peanut butter brings to your life is likely not worth the extra effort it took to find it.

Find the Right Motivation

While many may see procrastination as a defect in personality, research is increasingly showing that it may actually just be a disconnect between the demands or rewards of a task and what motivates the procrastinator. In other words, it's possible that procrastinators are not inherently lazy or useless individuals; rather, they're simply faced with tasks which do not match their skill levels or personal motivations.

When it comes to skill levels, procrastinators may find themselves either overly qualified or grossly inadequate for the task at hand. If they find a task too easy, they get bored, and thus procrastinate as they seek the thrill of leaving a task to the last minute in order to "up the ante." If they find a task too demanding or difficult, they feel overwhelmed, and thus procrastinate as they seek to avoid the pressure of having to surmount an impossible challenge.

Procrastination can also arise out of a mismatch between the rewards of a task and what motivates procrastinators. Procrastinators tend to be intrinsically rather than extrinsically motivated. This means that extrinsic motivation, such as dangling a carrot in front of them or threatening to beat them with a stick on their behinds, isn't likely to push procrastinators into action.

Rather, they are moved into action by intrinsic motivation—the inherent joy and pleasure they derive from doing a task, whether or not they're rewarded by money or praise for doing it, and whether or not they're punished by salary deductions and ridicule for failing to do it. In other words, to spur themselves into action, procrastinators have to *want* to do something.

So if you're one to procrastinate, the answer to stopping that habit may not be in clinging to a task's rewards and punishments, but rather, in focusing on what you truly value and enjoy doing. If you're intrinsically motivated to do something, you won't need to drag yourself to do it every single time. Instead, you'll look forward to doing it and feel an energy surge enough to help you kick-start action and persist in completing that task.

Does this mean you should only elect to do tasks you find valuable or enjoyable and reject doing the rest? Not necessarily; this is reality, after all. The key is in finding aspects of every task or project that you can care about. It's all a matter of perspective. Since no one else's reasons or persuasions can make you get to work, you'll just have to create your own reasons for doing a task. Look for aspects in it that you enjoy or that show you what makes it worthwhile, and focus on those.

Suppose you're with a team tasked to spearhead your company's tree-planting initiative. You're not that keen to get down and dirty digging holes and planting seedlings, so at first glance you find the entire project uninteresting and you put off working on it. However, upon a closer examination of what the project entails, as well as your own personal interests and values, you discover a match. You learn that the project needs someone to research the kinds of trees that would grow well in a particular location, and such a researching task is right up your alley. Discovering that connection, you now feel energized to work on the project and can't wait to get started.

Another example is when you have to review company records for a financial audit and you find that though you hate the tedium of sorting through a sea of documents, you love the fact-finding and problem-solving side of it. You start to think of it as an opportunity to "play detective," something you've always enjoyed doing—

thus, you find a renewed sense of enthusiasm to do the task.

So by discovering an aspect of the project you're intrinsically motivated to do, you're less likely to procrastinate and you get to put in effort without needing to drag yourself to do it. Your intrinsic motivations, interests, and values are all clues to what will unleash the energy and talents you have toward productive ends.

Once you're able to tap that energy by proactively seeking to connect aspects of a task to what really motivates you, not only will you find it easier to fight procrastination, you'll also find it harder to *not* work on that task which now tugs at your heart.

So there you have it—the three main approaches to cultivate anti-procrastination mindsets: (1) master the physics of productivity, (2) eliminate the paradox of choice, and (3) find the right motivation for yourself.

Let's go back to something we mentioned earlier in the book as a major cause of procrastination: simple fear.

This notion is parallel to what we call "planning paralysis"—when planning becomes a higher priority than actually *doing* something. The job of *planning* to leave your comfort zone takes precedence over, or at least valuable time from, your actual project.

Ultimately, it's another form of procrastination. Gathering more information than you absolutely need, conducting multiple analyses of different ways to achieve something, combing over minute and usually unnecessary details, debating back and forth in your own head about multiple scenarios—all of these actions are used as something that will postpone your taking action. After all, it's easier to plan than do.

Planning in itself is a comfort zone, and not just because you can do it from a couch. To do something, you have to get outside and risk a certain vulnerability. So it's always easier to keep planning, because technically it's useful to your task.

You can lead yourself to believe you're being productive toward your overall goal. Planning to map out precision and sewing up random details isn't the worst way to go about projects. But more often, planning is a device that helps one avoid action to mollify our fears and anxieties. When we're spinning our wheels, it's because we've started listening to that inner voice that likes to harangue us into believing all we do will fail and we're foolish for trying. Keep in mind that over-planning is an often redundant process that people hide behind.

As a member of the human race, the tendency for procrastination may be hardwired into your limbic system, but that doesn't mean you should forever be a slave to your own primitive drives and impulses. Building and fortifying these three mindsets will turn you into an individual in better control of those drives and impulses, so you can beat the lure of procrastination and instead determinedly move toward more productive ends.

Takeaways:

- Procrastination may be a reflection of battling biological forces, and we can swing the battle in our favor if we use some of the mindset tactics in this chapter. Fear is an understated underlying cause for procrastination.
- The first such tactic is to understand how Newton's three laws of physics can apply to procrastination. Viewing your productivity (or lack thereof) as an equation is helpful, because it allows you to think through the variables present in your life and learn how to manipulate them. First, an object at rest tends to stay at rest, while an object in motion tends to stay in motion (the first step is the hardest step). Next, the amount of work produced is a product of the focus and the force that is applied toward it

(focus your efforts intentionally). Finally, for every action, there is an equal and opposite reaction (take inventory of the productive and unproductive forces present in your life).

- Another factor in procrastination is the paradox of choice, wherein choices and options are actually detrimental because they cause indecision and plague us with doubt. They might even cause us to act like Buridan's donkey and proverbially starve to death between two dishes of food. To combat this, get into the habit of setting a time limit on your decisions, making matters black and white, aiming to become satisficed, and immediately picking a default option.
- Finally, finding the right motivation can be important. It's not that you should only do things that you feel motivation for, but rather, you can find bits and pieces of what motivates you and what you value in everything you do. It's just a matter of looking.

Chapter 4: Psychological Tactics

"Procrastination is the grave in which opportunity is buried."
—Anonymous

How do you get a machine to work?

You need to plug it to an energy source and push the right buttons. Now, getting yourself to work wouldn't be quite as simple as that, but in a way, you also have "energy sources" you can plug into and psychological "buttons" you can push to get yourself to be more productive and avoid procrastinating. If you know where to tap the energy to power yourself through tasks and which buttons to push—or avoid pushing—to get yourself to work, then you'll be able to beat procrastination and be well on your way toward achieving your goals.

This chapter will introduce you to three psychological tactics that'll have you push just the right buttons in your own psyche, so you can get yourself up and running as you set about accomplishing your tasks. These three tactics are: (1) don't rely on your mood, (2) deal with omission bias, and (3) visualize your future self.

Don't Rely on Your Mood

How many times have you put off a task just because you're "not yet in the mood" to work on it, or because you "don't feel like working"? What's your record for the length of time you've waited to "feel the right moment to start" before you actually set about on a task?

If you're a constant procrastinator, you've probably lost track of the count already (Hint: you're never in the mood to do something you don't want).

So as a psychological tactic to counter this tendency, consider changing up things to work the other way around: Instead of waiting for your mood to spark you into action, act first in order to spark your mood into a motivated, all-systems-go mode. In other words, start operating under the notion that the right action inspires the right mood, instead of the other way around.

For example, whether or not you feel in the mood to research that project you're supposed to do, sit yourself down and start browsing a page on the subject. Soon enough, you'll find yourself gaining more and more momentum, and you'll feel more and more motivated to keep with the task.

No matter what mood you're in—happy or cranky, excited or bored, calm or edgy—just start. No doubt you've noticed this to be a theme of the book. Often, you'll be pleasantly surprised to discover that it's only after you get to work that your mood switches into just the right gear to keep you working. If you only waited for the right mood to come upon you and never bothered to lift a finger until it did, you would never have gotten yourself to a point when you actually feel like working.

You're essentially waiting for divine intervention, a miracle, or a flash of inspiration—very risky and ephemeral things to build a reliance upon. Starting, however, is something you can control.

Okay, you get that you need to stop waiting for your mood to shape up by itself and now need to take matters into your own hands. What do you do? You can't just take a bunch of tools and repair yourself to get working, right?

Researchers have designed a playbook of strategies to help you repair your mood by the very actions you take. The added benefit to mastering this playbook is that not only will it help you take action no matter what mood you're in, it will also equip you with strategies to repair your mood in general. So whether it's your intention to kick the procrastination bug out of your system or to simply convert negative feelings into positive ones, practice the three psychological tricks described below to experience a mood boost whenever you need one.

First, set a low threshold for getting started. As advised by Dr. Timothy Pychyl, a leading researcher in the field of procrastination, making the threshold for getting started relatively low can trick your mind into getting motivated for a task. The low threshold suggests to you that the task is completely manageable, and anticipating that you'll easily get past the first hurdle of the task will help you boost positive emotions in relation to the work you need to do.

By increasing the positive feelings you associate with a task, you'll be more likely to jump in on it.

So if, say, you need to create a PowerPoint presentation of your company profile, decide to first work on just the titles of each slide. Leave the actual detail for later; it's not pertinent to your current threshold and goal of just getting started. That way, you'll be more motivated, knowing the simplest task is up first.

Second, Dr. Pychyl suggests that you "time travel."

Don't worry, this book hasn't taken a turn to sci-fi-ville. Time travel here pertains to the practice of projecting yourself into the future as a way to anticipate how good you'd feel if you finish a task, and how bad you'd feel if you don't. Vividly think about your future self and how they will feel. This strategy remedies the tendency to get so caught up in your present anxieties—or present pleasures—such that you fail to appreciate the relief and sense of fulfilment that comes once you accomplish a task, and the horror that comes if you don't.

For example, if you're not feeling motivated to work on a speech you've been asked to do, picture yourself already up on that podium. How would it go if you went into it well-prepared? On the other hand, how might you sound if you failed to prepare for it well enough?

Picture the pain and the triumph and use those feelings as a mental boost. The image of you making a fool out of yourself in front of a large crowd if you failed at that task might just be the push you need to start working on that speech now.

Third, forgive yourself for procrastinating.

One way that you get overpowered by procrastination is by letting yourself think that your past procrastination slip-ups are irredeemable, and that they have done such irreparable damage that you might as well give up on trying to remedy the situation altogether. You feel guilty and blame yourself for being too weak to fight off procrastination, so you get discouraged trying to do the task any longer.

For instance, you may think that because you've procrastinated on doing that research project for the past hour, any attempt to start researching now is already a lost cause, so you decide to spend the rest of the evening just procrastinating. When you forgive yourself, you stop thinking in terms of lost causes, move past wallowing in self-pity, and move to the next phase, which is action.

Instead of wallowing in that bottomless pit of self-blame and guilt, resolve to forgive yourself for procrastinating and pick up the motivation to start anew once you recognize you've slipped up. As associate psychology professor, Michael Wohl, found in their 2010 study, university freshmen who forgave themselves for putting off studying for the first exam procrastinated less on the next exam. Forgiving yourself for procrastinating thus decreases the likelihood of you later procrastinating on your tasks.

Deal with Omission Bias

If we know procrastinating is bad for us, why do we still keep doing it? As previously discussed, biological explanations point to the roles of the limbic system running wild with primitive drives and impulses, and the prefrontal cortex not being strong or skilled enough to get those drives and impulses under control.

But what about the psychological explanation for our proclivity for doing something that causes problems for us? What is it in our human psyche and cognitive processes that predisposes us to put off tasks to later, even when we know we should really be doing them now?

According to business site Harvard Business Review, we can chalk it up to what is known as *omission bias*. Omission bias is a cognitive distortion by which we fail to see the consequences of *not* doing something. While it's easy for us to envision the consequences of committing something bad, it's harder for us to imagine the costs of omission. This is because when we perform or witness an action, we are primed to anticipate an effect that arises out of that action. We wait to see what happens afterwards. But when there's no tangible action, our minds find no reason to try to see how that might change things for us.

We tend to just go about our lives not even thinking of omission as possibly having effects, precisely because we think there wasn't an action to cause any effects in the first place. Essentially, out of sight, out of mind.

For instance, it tends to be easier for us to picture how frequently eating a load of greasy fast food meals is going to risk our heart health, but it's harder for us to recognize how *not* exercising can place us at the same health risk. While we may actively avoid those oily take-out in an attempt to maintain a healthy lifestyle, we aren't as likely to start an exercise regimen to support that same goal. It just doesn't have the same psychological impact.

Omission bias is often at play when we procrastinate on tasks. See, procrastination is essentially an omission—it's the phenomenon of *not* doing our intended tasks. Owing to our bias against considering the pros and cons of not doing things, we tend to feel less alarmed by our procrastination tendencies. Because technically, we're not doing anything, our minds take that to mean we can't possibly be doing anything wrong.

Our minds reason, *"How can we be doing anything wrong if we're literally not doing anything?"* Such is the brilliant "logic" of our mind, bending reason to support our procrastination habits so we get to continue reaping short-term pleasures while blind to the negative impacts of our inaction.

So how do you get out of the rut that omission bias creates for you? The answer starts with awareness. Once you're better aware of the gravity of consequences attached to not doing a task, you'll also be more motivated to start doing that task. Recognize how omission bias tends to operate in your life, how it has sabotaged your motivation to work on tasks in the past, and how it's likely to affect your future decisions and actions.

Proactively magnifying the negative effects of omission bias on your life is a powerful way to confront it, and a key strategy to transition from procrastination to productivity. There may not be any immediate negative effects, but as you start to think outwards from yourself and into the future, more and more will materialize. More than simple awareness is needed from time to time.

For example, say you've been putting off your task of reviewing and updating your company's current policies and procedures on chemical disposal. If you aren't aware of your own omission bias, you'll likely feel as if you're not really doing anything wrong, because there's a current system in place that's working anyway. However, you're conveniently ignoring the negative impact that *not* doing that task might carry, including health risks for everyone in the community.

Continuing to employ outdated chemical disposal methods may be poisoning your neighborhood's water supply or hazarding the health of all company employees, including your own. But without proactively imagining these negative effects of inaction, you'll be less likely to feel the urge to act. To remedy the situation, reconsider the negative consequences of not doing the task at hand and use it to motivate yourself to get working.

Visualize your Future Self

Remember that the defining feature of procrastination isn't just the act of putting off tasks; it's the deliberate delaying of intended tasks, even while knowing full well that such delay will cause negative consequences in the future. Well, guess who suffers in that scenario?

Procrastination isn't just about complacency or mere forgetfulness. It's more about hazarding the welfare of our future selves as we focus on gaining short-term pleasure at the cost of long-term benefits.

Research into chronic procrastination has unearthed an interesting discovery on what sets apart chronic procrastinators from the rest. We each have a way of transporting our mind into the future—we do it whenever we set goals, plan, or bring up positive affirmations. Through these activities, we're able to connect with our future selves and visualize how we're going to transition from our present situation to that future vision.

For chronic procrastinators, though, that vision of their future selves tends to be blurry, more abstract, and impersonal.

They often feel an emotional disconnect between who they are at present and who they'll become in the future. Thus, they have a harder time delaying gratification. As they are more strongly in tune with the desires of their present selves and don't feel connected enough with their future selves to care about their welfare, chronic procrastinators thus more readily give in to the lure of short-term pleasures.

Rather than sacrifice present comfort for future rewards, they choose to revel in what feels good now because their vision tends to be more limited to the immediate moment.

This is what psychology professor Dr. Fuschia Sirois calls *temporal myopia* (more easily thought of as nearsightedness with regards to time)—a key quality that may largely underlie chronic procrastination.

To further clarify the phenomenon of how our perception of time can influence the way we make decisions, Hal Hershfield, a professor of marketing at UCLA's Anderson School of Management, conducted experiments. Using virtual reality, Hershfield had people interact with their future self.

The results of his experiments revealed that people who interacted with their future selves were more likely to be concerned about both their present and future selves, and also tended to act favorably in consideration of their future selves. For instance, they were much more likely to put money in a fake, experiment-based retirement account for the benefit of the future self they interacted with.

What did Hershfield's studies show us? The better we're able to visualize and interact with our future self, the better we get at taking good care of it.

This is because by visualizing and connecting with our future self, we feel the reality of the upcoming circumstances and recognize how the actions of our present self are bound to create a real impact on our future self. For example, if we visualize how failing to prepare well for a seminar we're tasked to organize would impact our future self and its reputation, we're more likely to feel motivated to start planning and acting now.

By practicing visualization, we start to see how procrastinating now may be good for our present self, but disastrous for our future self. As we empathize with the fate of our future self, and the kind of life it will have to live through if we keep the habit of procrastination up (e.g., sleepless nights trying to get caught up with work, turning in haphazardly-done output, having to deal with career failures), we begin to feel motivated to change our present ways to be more productive.

So the next time you're feeling drawn to procrastinate, think of your future self. Create a vivid image in your mind depicting your future self in a failure scenario, and try to feel what they feel in that event.

Then picture your future self in a success scenario, and also try to feel all the positive emotions you'd feel in that moment. Visualize every little step and reaction your future self would make in both situations. Getting a taste of the two alternate lives your future self might experience will increase your motivation to act toward realizing your success vision rather than the failure depiction. Make it stick and make it impactful.

As you come to appreciate the beauty of a success scenario, visualize how the completed task looks like, and trace your way back—that is, outline the specific tasks you need to perform to get to that vision of your future self proudly completing the task at hand and reaping its rewards. If you still feel hindered from getting started toward your goal, try to review which of the smaller subtasks is holding you up and why.

As you troubleshoot your lack of motivation to get going, always keep the vision of your future self at the forefront of your mind. It will serve as a reminder both of the positive consequences of beating procrastination, and of the negative impacts of failing to fight the urge to delay your intended tasks.

In conclusion, learn to push the right psychological "buttons" for you to rid yourself of procrastination and become a more productive individual. As you master the art of repairing your mood, confronting your omission bias, and visualizing your future self, you'll get to have less and less of a problem getting yourself to start up and get going until your tasks are completed. Yes, as a human being with your own set of drives and impulses, you may never get yourself to work as simply as you can turn a machine on.

But with the right psychological tactics, you can achieve a mastery of yourself well enough to be able to manage those drives and impulses and steer yourself toward productivity and maximum efficiency.

Takeaways:

- Sometimes it's necessary to trick ourselves into doing what we don't want to. In fact, that's a primary aspect of improving and practicing anything. We are momentarily seduced by the benefit or end result to the point where we can grin and bear the present pain.
- Many of us think we can only work when are in the mood for it, or when inspiration strikes us. That is a losing battle. Don't rely on your mood to get you where you want to go. Instead, think the opposite way: Once you begin action, your mood will follow. Forgive yourself for procrastinating, because that

prevents you from a negative spiral and giving up altogether.

- Understand and tame omission bias. This is when you realize that it's easy to feel the impact from doing something, but not the impact from skipping something. This is about more than awareness; you can battle omission bias with proactive visualization of the bad future you are creating. That will kick you into gear.

- Finally, visualize your future self. Most of us suffer from *temporal myopia,* which is when you as nearsighted with regards to time. Specifically, you don't think about your future self; when you can effectively visualize your future self in excruciating detail, you are more aware of what you need to do and more impacted by it—because you recognize that you are your own future!

Chapter 5: Strategic Planning

"You don't have to see the whole staircase, just take the first step."
—Martin Luther King, Jr.

When it comes to beating procrastination, half the battle is getting a good strategy in place. If you plan your tasks well and set up your workload strategically, you can strip away the chances of slipping into procrastination. No more delaying the start of a project, straying off task, or getting tempted into engaging in mindless, unimportant activities—rather, you can structure things to set yourself up for productivity, efficiency, and achievement.

This chapter will teach you four strategic planning tactics to preempt procrastination before it even begins: (1) use the STING method, (2) focus on the process, rather than the product, (3) manipulate variables in the "procrastination equation," (4) pit your hated tasks against each other, and (5) use temptation bundling.

Use the STING method

The STING method represents an acronym of five strategies you can implement in order to prevent procrastination. It stands for **S**elect one task, **Time** yourself, **I**gnore everything else, **N**o breaks, and **G**ive yourself a reward.

S - Select one task. In order to avert procrastination, focus is the name of the game. And when there is more than one task in front of you, your focus will tend to be divided as well. Instead of immediately starting on a task, you'll be led to ask yourself, "*Should I do Task A, Task B, or Task C first? How about I find a way to do them all at once? Or how about I put off doing any of them at all?*" Being overwhelmed by numerous tasks in front of you can be a precursor to procrastination, as having to make a decision paralyzes you from taking action. Also, having a large goal with no clear, smaller subtasks you can easily work on can be off-putting. Not knowing how or where to start, you may instead succumb to procrastination and opt for other enjoyable activities instead.

To remedy the situation, select a single, small task on which you should focus at a particular time. With a clear course of action laid out in front of you, you'll be less likely to try to escape an overwhelming or confusing situation by procrastination.

T - Time yourself. One notion that often breeds procrastination is the thought of having to work on a task for endless, punishing hours. With such a gloomy forecast of how your life might look in the near future if you jump into the task at hand, you'll be likely to opt for delaying the task instead. In other words, when you can't see light at the end of the tunnel, it's a normal response for you to avoid entering that tunnel in the first place—that is, to procrastinate. Because what's the point of troubling yourself with a task when you can't see an end to it anyway?

Timing yourself is a good strategy to counter the threat of procrastination in this situation. Timing yourself means setting a predetermined amount of time you'll be spending on a particular task. Give yourself, say, one hour to work on that business proposal, and promise to stop once the hour is up regardless of whether you've finished the task.

That way, you'll be more motivated to start working on it, because you can see the "light at the end of the tunnel"—a respite from the labor at the end of the hour. Moreover, you'll be better driven to work more efficiently because you know you only have so much time to spend on that task. You'll want to make each minute count, as the countdown ignites in you a sense of urgency and competition against the clock (or yourself), pushing you to move while the time still allows it.

I - Ignore everything else. As you're doing the task in the moment, focus only on that task and ignore everything else. This is easier to do when you've selected only one task and have timed yourself, as these first two strategies allow you to narrow down your focus and reassure you that you can bother with other tasks, or indulge in distractions, as soon as the time you've set is up.

In the meantime, you need to focus solely on the task you've selected and put your blinders on, ignoring everything else unrelated to the task at hand. It's understandably very hard to be able to pull that off without slipping, especially when you're used to indulging the distractions all around you. However, the moment you do manage to completely ignore everything else and simply focus on the task, you will experience an incredible clarity and sense of self-assurance.

You discover that you do have it in you to stand your ground as you ignore extraneous stuff, and that the world didn't end when you chose to disregard all the distractions around you.

For example, if you've committed to accomplishing an activity report within the next hour, focus solely on that and ignore everything else—whether it's thoughts about the next thing on your to-do list, or environmental distractors as your mobile phone, your email alerts, and your chatty colleague. Ignoring these shields you from the extraneous stuff that detract you from your purpose and thus prevents you from procrastinating.

N - No breaks. Within the time frame you've set for focusing on a task, make sure you refrain from taking breaks. Breaks are necessary to revive your energy levels and recharge your mental stamina, but they shouldn't be taken willy-nilly. If you've planned your schedule effectively, you should already have scheduled breaks at appropriate times throughout the day, so any other breaks in the midst of ongoing workhours are unwarranted.

While scheduled breaks keep you on track by being strategic, reenergizing methods of self-reinforcement, unscheduled breaks derail you from your goal, as they offer you opportunities to procrastinate by making you feel as if you've got "free time."

Taking unscheduled breaks is a surefire way to fall into the procrastination trap. You may rationalize that you're only getting a cup of coffee to keep yourself alert, but in reality, you're just trying to avoid having to work on a task at your desk. You start off by getting that cup of coffee, but the next thing you know, you're already happily chattering away at the next cubicle, or enjoying

YouTube binge-watching in a corner. Once you allow yourself unplanned breaks, you'll be more likely to find yourself captive to procrastination. So to prevent procrastination, commit to having no random breaks instead.

G - Give yourself a reward. Once you're done with a task, reward yourself. Indulge in a favorite snack, treat yourself to a movie, or snuggle down to a good nap. This tactic deters procrastination because it pulls you forward into starting and completing a task by promising something pleasurable at the end. Remember that humans are creatures hardwired to avoid pain and pursue pleasure.

While this same mechanism can lure you into procrastination, it can also be hacked to keep you away from procrastination—and that is by promising to give yourself a reward upon achieving your goal on time. That way, you're giving yourself an extra incentive for accomplishing the task, and the anticipation of that reward will motivate you to power through the work needed to attain it.

Focus on the Process, Not the Product

Have you ever felt discouraged from embarking on a task upon seeing the sheer massiveness of what you need to accomplish? Maybe instead of pushing through with the task, you've opted to put it off instead, as you have become engulfed by the fear of not having enough in you to see the task through.

This is how procrastination is born out of a focus on the end product. As you set your sights and focus only on the loftiest goal, its height can overwhelm you, and you begin to doubt your capacity to reach it. So instead of starting to work toward it, you fill your time with delaying tactics, from the shameless playing of mobile games to the more surreptitious over-planning paralysis.

Try to focus on the process rather than the product. While product pertains to the outcome of your efforts, process refers to the actions you take and the flow of time that passes as you work toward that outcome.

If you've ever witnessed or heard how the Japanese conduct tea ceremonies—how every step of the ceremony has significance, and is thus done with utmost care and respect—you'll easily recognize what a focus on process rather than product looks like. For the Japanese, tea ceremonies aren't done just so one can produce and fill their bellies with tea.

Rather, the ceremonies are done for their own sake—the process itself has more significance than the product does. And when you focus on the process and dedicate your full attention to it, the product inevitably comes as a result of that process—the tea gets made and drank in the end.

Now, how does this relate to procrastination? When you need to do something, especially if it's a large task, it's easy to get overwhelmed by the pressure of having to deliver the product.

This pressure is usually enough for people to opt for procrastination instead of taking on that task. To avoid this, try to focus on the process of doing that task. What do you need to do in order to get the job done? Break things down into smaller tasks, then schedule these tasks to be done within chunks of time spread out over days or weeks.

These smaller tasks are easier to swallow mentally, and the bite-sized portions relieve you of pressure by allowing you to focus just on one particular work block at a time, rather than allowing you to get intimidated by the idea of an overarching goal.

For example, suppose you need to devise a handbook intended for visitors who come by your company. The handbook is your product. Thinking about this product in its entirety—must include everything from company background, vision and mission, organizational chart, and safety reminders for visitors—can trigger overwhelming feelings of dread about having to undertake such a mammoth task.

So instead of focusing on the product (i.e., the entire handbook), focus on the process of creating that product section by section. Assign yourself only one section for a particular chunk of time—say, piecing together the organizational chart for this hour.

Do the next section at another scheduled time, and so on, until you complete the entire thing. Keep your eyes focused on what's in front of you and just complete your tasks. By focusing on a section-by-section approach, you get to ease into the process and feel that you're accomplishing things throughout, instead of experiencing a sense of success only at the end of it.

Think of this strategy as similar to building a structure brick by brick. You'll be better motivated to start working and keep going when you know you just have a specific number of bricks to lay at a time, rather than expecting yourself to plop down a huge structure all at once.

Because you have no unrealistic expectations of yourself, you're also saved from having to feel an overwhelming amount of pressure to accomplish the impossible. You get to pace yourself well and don't feel guilty about "just laying 10 bricks for the day," because you're well aware of the fact that those "10 bricks" constitute enough work that'll still allow you to achieve your goal on time.

Manipulate the "Procrastination Equation"

Yes, you read that right—someone has formulated an equation of procrastination, one that elegantly works out the interaction of variables that make procrastination more likely to occur.

That someone is Piers Steel, a leading researcher on procrastination. While James Clear applied Newton's three laws of motion to the mechanisms of productivity, Steel distilled and synthesized 691 studies on the subject to come up with a comprehensive, evidence-based equation that explains motivation and procrastination.

Known as the "procrastination equation," Steel drew up the formula as follows:

$$Motivation = \frac{Expectancy \times Value}{Impulsiveness \times Delay}$$

In the equation, motivation pertains to your drive to do your intended task. The higher your motivation, the less likely you're going to procrastinate. The lower your motivation, the more likely you're going to procrastinate.

As shown in the equation, your level of motivation depends on four variables: (1)

expectancy, (2) value, (3) impulsiveness, and (4) delay.

Expectancy refers to your expectation of succeeding at the task. For example, if you need to deliver a sales presentation, expectancy pertains to how much you expect the presentation to be success, as evidenced by your client buying your product, or simply by your effective delivery of the presentation.

Note that the expectancy variable is at the numerator of the equation. This means that the higher your expectancy of success, the more motivated you're going to be to work on your task.

Value pertains to the importance, worth, or pleasantness of the task to you. How much does your intended task matter to you? How much do you like doing that task? Your answers to these questions speak of the value you attach to the task. If the sales presentation you're about to do matters very much to you, and/or you actually like working on a sales presentation, then you're more likely to be motivated to get going on it. Like the expectancy variable, the value variable is also at the numerator of the equation, which means the more you value the task, the greater your motivation for doing it is.

Now let's talk about the two variables at the denominator of the equation: impulsiveness and delay.

Impulsiveness refers to your tendency to act on your impulses immediately, without first thinking through their consequences. The more impulsive you are, the more likely you tend to follow your desires and urges at the drop of a hat. From this description, you can imagine just how being impulsive is related to procrastinating.

For example, let's say that in the middle of preparing for your sales presentation, you feel the urge to check on your social media accounts. If you have an impulsive personality, you'll feel strongly compelled to act on that urge, thus lowering your motivation to focus on the task and leading you to procrastinate instead. This is the reason why impulsiveness is at the denominator of the procrastination equation. Its relationship with motivation is inverse: The more impulsive you are, the less motivated you'll be to work on your intended task.

Finally, there's the variable called delay.

Delay pertains to the interval of time between your completion of a task and your receipt of the reward for doing so. For instance, suppose you've been told that the cash incentive for successfully delivering your sales presentation wouldn't be given to you until your retirement. How would you feel about working on that presentation now?

Such a long delay between your task completion and its reward is likely to decrease your motivation for working on it. The longer you expect to wait for the payoff, the more difficult it is for you to push yourself to get going on the task. This is why the delay variable is at the denominator of the equation. Like impulsiveness, its relationship with motivation is inverse: The greater the delay of the reward, the lesser motivation you'll feel to work on the task.

In summary, here is what's at work when it comes to procrastination: The more you expect to succeed and the more you value a task, the more you're motivated to work on it, and therefore, the less likely you're going to procrastinate. On the other hand, the more impulsive you are and the more delayed the payoff for the task is, the less you're motivated to work, and therefore, the more likely it is that you're going to procrastinate.

And now to answer the million-dollar question: How do you manipulate those variables to beat procrastination?

The beauty of arranging the components of procrastination as variables in a mathematical equation is that you get to clearly see which components you need to increase and which you need to decrease. Let's take a look at the general equation again:

$$Motivation = \frac{Expectancy \times Value}{Impulsiveness \times Delay}$$

Given the equation, the formula for increasing motivation—and therefore, decreasing procrastination—is simple: Increase the numerators (expectancy and value) and decrease the denominators (impulsiveness and delay).

You may choose to implement a combination of those techniques to increase your motivation, depending on what best applies to your situation.

For example, if you already have high expectations of success and attach a high value to the task, but tend to be highly impulsive and easily give in to temptations, then you know you've got to work on decreasing the impulsiveness variable—so maybe try to eliminate distractions in your environment and practice being more thoughtful rather than being overly reactive.

If you aren't impulsive, but tend to procrastinate because you lack self-confidence and expect failure, then work on increasing your expectancy for success by working to discover your strengths and learning how to apply them to succeed in your task.

Let's consider how manipulating the procrastination equation would look like applied to our earlier scenario of being tasked to deliver a sales presentation. Remember that given the variables in the procrastination equation—expectancy, value, impulsiveness, and delay—there are at least four ways you can go about increasing your motivation to work on this task.

First, increase your expectancy of success. Put simply, you need to be more optimistic. Think positive! Concrete strategies to help you do so include watching motivational videos, calling to mind situations in the past in which you've succeeded, and engaging in visualization.

Believe in your capacity to do the presentation well, and visualize a scene in which your audience is interested and captivated by your presentation and your client reacts positively to your pitch. To prevent this visualization from being just a daydream, though, researchers suggest employing a technique called mental contrasting.

After imagining your presentation going well, mentally contrast that with the actual situation you're in right now. How much work have you really done at this point to be able to realize that vision? This technique is effective at jumpstarting planning and action, driving you to move yourself from your current situation to a successful outcome.

Second, increase the value of the task to you. If doing a sales presentation is something you already highly value because you find it worthwhile or enjoyable, then you don't need to do much more other than continually remind yourself of why it's valuable to you. But if doing the presentation is something you dislike or find meaningless, then your task is to find an aspect of it you could like, or to create meaning in the task.

The art of self-motivation has a lot to do with managing your own perceptions. To increase task value, you may consider how doing that sales presentation well could have repercussions on your career progression, and ultimately, your quality of life. Reframe the task not as an end in itself, but a means to an end you value, and you'll find yourself better motivated to get going on it.

Third, decrease your level of impulsiveness. While some people tend to be inherently more impulsive than others, everyone can implement strategies to decrease their overall impulsiveness.

These strategies will need you to modify and structure your environment in such a way that you'll have fewer opportunities to act on your impulses. Suggested by Steel, this approach needs you to "throw away the key." For instance, while working on your sales presentation, close all other tabs on your computer that may tempt you to procrastinate (e.g., YouTube, Facebook, Instagram pages). Don't work in front of the TV.

Eat a good meal before sitting down to work so that you won't be tempted to get up for snack time again while you're working.

Finally, decrease the delay of the reward after task completion. While this variable is less likely to be in your control than the other components (e.g., you're usually not the one who has a say on when you're going to get compensated), there are still ways you can tweak this variable to your advantage. For instance, break down the task into smaller subtasks and reward yourself for completing each of those subtasks.

That way, you can keep feeding your motivation with little reinforcements throughout the process of working on that larger task. Think of it as continuing to feed the fire with small sticks in order to keep it burning. In making your presentation, for instance, reward yourself with a nice meal or a movie when you complete a subtask, such as completing the presentation outline.

By knowing how to steer each of the equation variables in just the right direction, you'll have the power to increase your motivation level and decrease your procrastination habits as you please.

Pit Hated Tasks Against Each Other

In the life of every procrastinator, there comes a time when all tasks appear either difficult or distasteful. If you've ever gone through such a time, you know just how challenging it is to get going on any task, no matter how much you try to increase your expectations for success, enhance the value of your tasks, speed up the process of gaining rewards, or manage your impulsiveness.

Because you hate all the tasks you need to do, you simply tend to slack off and prefer instead to get steamrolled by deadlines.

During such times, how do you make yourself get off your butt and start working?

The solution is in the problem itself—make your hated tasks compete against each other. Construct a to-do list, but make it your mission to include only tasks that you consider hateful, daunting, or even downright impossible. At the very top of the list, put in tasks that sound important, but really aren't, and appear to have deadlines, but really don't. For example, you may include such tasks as replacing all the file folders with new ones that are labeled in a uniform way, or proofreading and then reprinting corrected versions of all of this month's reports.

Then, lower on the list, include a couple of unpleasant, yet important and totally doable tasks—say, preparing the quarterly accounting report, writing out and disseminating the minutes of the previous meeting, and conducting a systems analysis. Since everything on your to-do list appears unpleasant and hateful to you anyway, you're bound to work on the tasks you hate the least just to avoid having to do the tasks you hate the most.

Because try and ask yourself—would you rather complete those important and doable tasks, or be forced to work on the more tedious tasks you included higher on your list? Chances are you'll be forced to opt for the lesser evil, so to speak. Thus, the irony—and the beauty—of this technique is that in any case, you'll end up procrastinating by being productive.

Temptation Bundling

Temptation bundling is the final way to kill procrastination and increase productivity by combining present and future selves and their conflicting needs.

Conceived by behavioral Katy Milkman at the University of Pennsylvania, temptation bundling is a way to blend both future and present self needs by making future rewards more immediate. You give yourself instant gratification in the present while also achieving goals that benefit your future self in the long-term. In our context, this is satisfying both the limbic system *and* the prefrontal cortex simultaneously.

It's simpler than it sounds.

If your goal is to satisfy the two versions of yourself (current and future), think about what that would require. Future self wants you to buckle down and take care of business so they are in a good position, or at least not suffering from your neglect. However, current self wants to engage in hedonism and enjoy the present moment.

Think eating Twinkies while working out, working out while watching TV, or doing work while soaking your feet in a salt bath—these are examples of ways to make the long-term feel good at the present moment, and this is the essence of temptation bundling. Bundle a temptation (current pleasure) with an unpleasurable activity (something you would otherwise procrastinate that your future self would be pleased to avoid), and you get the best of both worlds.

There is no need to suffer in the present to get something done for your future self; if you do suffer, then you will lose all motivation and procrastinate. So find ways to bundle your temptations with your long-term goals. In other words, pair your obligations with instantaneous rewards.

Milkman found that up to 51% of her study participants were willing to exercise with temptation bundling. It is an effective means to correct procrastination habits. You should make a list with two columns, one side being your guilty pleasures or temptations and the other side being things you need to do for your future self. Then figure out creative ways to link the two conflicting columns in harmony.

Suppose you like chocolate, surfing, soccer, and running. But work, homework, and piano lessons stand in your way.

Chocolate	Homework
Surfing	Work
Soccer	Piano Lessons

How might you combine things to make the unpleasurable more tolerable? There are at least nine combinations between these elements, and nine different ways you can bundle temptations. How might you combine chocolate with homework, soccer with work, and surfing with piano lessons? It doesn't take long to imagine how you can bribe yourself into doing exactly what you need to do.

Takeaways:

- Even though we know procrastination is always lurking, we can't always fight it, no matter how close attention we pay. That's why it pays to structure your day and work to avoid procrastination completely. At least you'll give yourself a much better fighting chance.
- First, you can use the STING method, by which you select one task, time yourself, ignore everything else, opt for no breaks, and give yourself a reward. It's the act of willful ignorance that makes STING so powerful. This is a scary concept, but once you resolve to only juggle one thing at a time, you'll be happy to report that the world didn't end.

- Secondly, rather than being pressured to achieve the end product as a whole, you can choose to focus on the process so you're better able to manage smaller chunks of work at a time. Just imagine the small tasks you have to do without thinking about the mountain you are tackling.
- Third, you can use your knowledge of the procrastination equation to your advantage by increasing both success expectancy and task value while decreasing reward delay and impulsiveness. You can manipulate each of these variables to increase your motivation and momentum toward productivity.
- Fourth, you can make your hated tasks compete against each other such that you'll tend to procrastinate on your most hated tasks by still being productive as you work on your less hated activities.
- Finally, you can bundle temptations. This essentially means to simultaneously satisfy the hedonist in

your current self and the prudence of your future self. Make both happy at the same time by pairing unpleasant tasks with sought-after pleasures.

Chapter 6: Structuring Against Procrastination

"Tomorrow is often the busiest day of the week."
—Anonymous

Procrastination can be like a ninja who creeps up on you and hijacks your entire day without you even noticing it. How can you prevent this from happening?

One of the major strategies you can employ is to structure your day and schedule with the goal in mind of beating procrastination before it hits you. Scheduling against procrastination may not work every time, but at least it gives you a guideline to act successfully. A number of ways this can be done is to: (1) aim for no more "zero days," (2) employ self-interrogation techniques, (3) use the "Ivy Lee method," and (4) write down a schedule.

Aim for no more "zero days"

A zero day is a day which you've let slip by without doing anything to achieve your goal. This concept may also apply to a week, an hour, or any other time segment you set (e.g., a zero year is one in which you probably hid out in a cave somewhere and hibernated for 365 days).

The concept of a zero day simplifies keeping score of how you're doing so far in working toward task completion or the achievement of your dreams. Think of life as a binary: Either you're doing something ("1"), or you're not ("0"). Aim for a string of 1s instead of 0s. Make it black and white with no in-between. In other words, see to it that every day, you do something that'll inch you closer to your goal.

Notice the phrase "inch you closer." The idea of having no more zero days doesn't mean you have to pack every single day with tasks that'll break new ground or catapult you to immediate success. This kind of thinking is what intimidates or scares most people away from doing anything at all to accomplish their goals.

They think they have to exhaust themselves with big, significant tasks every day because they believe simply pecking at something is not worth the effort.

Then, overwhelmed by the idea of having to start on a large task in front of them, they procrastinate and build a string of 0s instead. Once they accumulate two to three days of 0s, they then find it easier to let the 0s persist for the rest of the days. They may think, *"Well, I've missed three days at the gym already, so what's the point of ever going at all when I can't be consistent with this?"* So they stop going to the gym. Others may think, *"I have to finish writing an entire chapter today. What's the point of sitting down to write if I'll add only two sentences in there?"* Then, intimidated by the thought of having to complete an entire chapter in one sitting, they simply procrastinate on the task and end up not writing a word in there at all.

So instead of seeing each day as either a 10 (task competed) or a 0 (no work done), replace the idea of needing a 10 to needing just a 1 (got something done). It doesn't matter how small a portion of a task you managed to do for the day; it only matters that you at least got something done.

Give yourself a 1 for the day. Strive to rid your calendar of any 0 in there, but if you do slip up and get a 0 one day, don't feel discouraged. Recover the next day with another 1. Once you get into the habit of doing something every single day toward your goal, the number of 0s in your calendar will start to get fewer until it finally disappears.

For instance, say you need to write a five-chapter research paper over the course of five months. Aim to complete at least one chapter a month, and pledge to have a string of non-zeroes every month.

This means that every single day, you need to get something down on paper or do something related to your research paper. Some days you may feel like an idea machine and jot down a lot of creative ways of looking at your research problem.

Other days you may feel demotivated, but still read even just a single paragraph of related literature. The only thing that matters is that you incur no zero days. It might also help motivate you if you reward yourself at the end of every month that you managed to get through without ever incurring a 0.

Another example is setting a "no zero before lunch" policy for yourself. This means that you should accomplish at least a little something toward your goal before every lunch hour.

The task you manage to complete may be as simple as scanning the documents needed for your database, or as complex as developing a software system validation procedure. Again, the only thing that matters is that you get something done, whether big or small. It's a way to break the inertia that will cause you to find comfort in procrastinating.

Keep in mind that you can apply the "no zero" policy to a whole range of time segments, from a span of hours to years. You may choose to commit to a "no zero hour," a "no zero day," a "no zero week," and so on. The important thing is that whatever time segment you set for yourself, you see to it that you get to do something within it that'll bring you closer to completing your task.

Employ self-interrogation techniques

The next time you find yourself being sweet-talked by a voice in your head saying you should just lay off on a task and instead do something more enjoyable, you know what you should do? Instead of trying to drown it out by arguments (or expletives, if you're feeling especially frustrated), Peter Banerjea suggests a more creative and effective solution: Ask it a question.

There are at least four questions you can keep at the ready to help you overcome procrastination the next time it tugs at you.

First, you may ask yourself, *"What one thing can I do to get started?"* Sometimes, you procrastinate mainly because you simply don't know where to start. Asking this question helps you recognize that the large task in front of you can be broken down into smaller sub-tasks, from which you can then select a single task to start with.

For instance, if you simply tell yourself you need to come up with an advertising plan for your product, you're more likely to procrastinate because you can't yet see the smallest possible units of action you can do to get going on that large task.

To remedy this, ask yourself what the most basic, smallest possible step you can do to start is. Maybe you realize you need to define your target market first, and the first small step toward doing that is getting a profile of your current customer base.

You have thus defined a single concrete task you can direct all your energy toward, instead of floundering about confused until you're tempted to procrastinate. Everything huge started with a tiny step—find your tiny step and gain momentum.

Second, try to answer, *"What are my three biggest priorities today?"* As in the first question, procrastination may just be the result of not knowing what to do because of the overwhelming number of tasks before you. By asking yourself to define your main priorities, you get to narrow down your focus and address specific activities.

You get to remind yourself of what's really essential to do for the day, and in so doing, you'll be better able to spot mere distractions and evade them. Keeping your biggest priorities at the forefront of your mind ensures the spotlight is on your intended tasks and not on extraneous activities.

Suppose you're flooded by a deluge of tasks preparing for your company's tenth founding anniversary. Instead of fleeing the anxiety-causing scene altogether, approach it by first asking yourself to name just three main things you need to do today. For instance, you may just aim to draft the guest list, pick out a theme, and decide on a catering service before the day ends.

Third, figure out, *"How can I make this easier?"* According to habit-building expert S. J. Scott, committing to something small and easy is one of the best ways to start building a new habit. So before you take on bigger goals, see if you can first incorporate bite-sized sections of it in your schedule. Make it as easy as possible and within the flow of your day; in fact, make it difficult to *not* comply.

For example, you might find it a daunting goal to finish reading 52 books in a year. To help kick-start yourself to read, ask yourself how you can make it easier for you to incorporate reading in your daily life. You may start with a goal of reading five pages every night before you go to sleep, then gradually build up the number of pages and the times of the day you do your reading.

You might download digital versions on to your phone and place the physical version on your shoes so that you cannot avoid them. You might also make rules for no television or Internet before you read. That way, you condition yourself to get into a more manageable habit before overwhelming yourself with an entire book each time.

And fourth, ask yourself, *"What will go wrong if I don't do this now?"* Think of the worst-case scenario from the time to time. Raising this question will help put things in perspective for you, especially as to how habitual procrastination can negatively impact your career and personal life. Inciting fear in yourself may not be the most positive emotional experience, but it can bring about positive results.

As you're reminded of how delaying tasks will ruin so many things for you, you'll feel more motivated to get started and keep going until you've reached your goal. By creating fear in yourself, you kick your own butt to stop bumming around and get going on things.

For instance, you might feel like procrastinating on a sales presentation you need to deliver for a potential client. To help overcome your impulse to procrastinate, consider what might go wrong if you don't get going on the task now. Really fall down the rabbit hole of potential consequences. You may leave yourself too little time to prepare adequately, which will lead you to give a horrible presentation. You might then lose that client, not to mention the confidence of your supervisor and colleagues.

This may snowball into you no longer being trusted with important tasks, spoiling your potential for professional growth and ascent on the career ladder. If you keep in mind how a single presentation can make or break the trajectory of your entire career, you'll feel a stronger motivation to stop procrastinating.

Use the "Ivy Lee method"

The Ivy Lee method is a prioritization strategy that will help you reach peak productivity and avoid procrastination. Ivy Lee was a well-known productivity consultant who helped steel magnate

Charles M. Schwab significantly improve the efficiency of his executive team in 1918. Schwab was so pleased with the positive impact of Lee's coaching on the progress of his company that he rewarded Lee a check worth $25,000, the equivalent of a $400,000 check in 2015.

What was the highly effective method Ivy Lee taught Schwab's executives to maximize productivity? It consists of five simple conditions.

First, at the end of every day, list the six most important things you should do the next day. It is important that you do not exceed listing six tasks. Second, rank those six items by order of importance. Consider how urgent and essential each task is and prioritize accordingly. Third, when you set out to start the following day, work only on the first thing on your list and don't stop until it's done. You're not allowed to move on to the second task until after you've finished the first.

Fourth, proceed with the rest of your list in like manner. Move any unfinished tasks to the new list of six tasks you set for the next day. And fifth, repeat this procedure every day.

For instance, say you have a number of things you wish to accomplish tomorrow, including answer some emails, prepare your notes for an upcoming work meeting, help your kid with a project, mow the lawn, do your taxes, and contact a repairman to do some home repairs.

For Step 1, you'll need to list these tasks down tonight. Then, notice that some of these tasks have clear and more urgent deadlines (e.g., the meeting has a set date) while others don't (e.g., you can put off mowing the lawn until the grass begins to cover your house).

This is where Step 2 comes in—rank the tasks in order of urgency and importance. While you may decide to rank "prepare meeting notes" first because the meeting happens in two days, you may put "mow the lawn" lower on your list.

When the following day arrives, move on to Step 3: Work on the first thing on your list and don't move on to the next until you're finished with the first. Thus, you'll be forced to complete your meeting notes first before doing anything else.

Once you're done with the first task, proceed to Step 4: Make your way down the list in the order you've set, not allowing yourself to skip to the next thing until the current task is completed.

Finally, for Step 5, sit yourself down at the end of the day and make a new to-do list for the next day, incorporating whatever unfinished tasks you have left on that new list.

You'll find that though the Ivy Lee method may seem deceptively simple, it's effective for a number of reasons. It eliminates the need for you to spend the first hour of your day wondering what you're going to do, and instead lays out your main task the night before so you hit the ground running the following day. It also forces you to commit to a set number of tasks per day, thus compelling you to figure out what's really necessary and what are mere distractions only. Procrastination only has the opportunity to sink its fangs into you when you have downtime to think—prevent this with the Ivy Lee method.

With clear priorities and goal posts set from the first hour and forward, you thus effectively cut your chances of slipping into procrastination born out of lack of direction and false notions about what's really essential. It's easier and more tempting to procrastinate when you're confused about which tasks to do first anyway. By affording you direction and clarity, the Ivy Lee method saves you from mindlessly falling into enjoyable, yet ultimately unimportant tasks.

Write Down a Schedule

How do you go about a typical workday? Do you arrive at the office with a clear idea about what you need to do, the resources you'll need for it, and when you're going to do it? Or do you simply freestyle through the day, picking up whatever task catches your eye, or waiting for others to usher you into one activity after another?

If you answered "yes" to the latter, then it's probably time for a major change. The science on productivity and efficiency at work indicates that having a schedule works better than simply winging it. In a study published by the *British Journal of Health Psychology*, just under 250 adults were assessed as to their motivation to exercise.

They were divided into three groups, all instructed to keep track of how often they exercised over the course of two weeks, but each given different conditions: [1] The control group was asked to read a few lines of a neutral book; [2] Group A (Motivation) was given a pamphlet outlining how exercise can decrease the risk for heart disease; and [3] Group B (Intention) was treated the same way as Group A, with the additional instruction to set a detailed exercise schedule over the course of two weeks. Group B identified when they would exercise, how long each workout would be, and where their workout would take place.

The outcome? While only 35% of Group A ended up working out once a week, 91% of Group B (those who scheduled their exercise) were able to accomplish the said routine. This goes to show how scheduling can dramatically improve your likelihood of following through on tasks with respect to a goal. So if scheduling is so helpful, how do you do it?

Scheduling involves identifying a number of elements. First, identify the tasks that you need to do. Second, decide when you're going to do each task. Assign a specific time frame (e.g., "from 8:30 AM to 9:30 AM") instead of using vague terms (e.g., "sometime in the morning").

Third, identify the tools and resources you'll need for the task so that you can prepare them beforehand. Fourth, name the physical location where you'll carry out each task. This way, you'll know exactly where to head to when the scheduled time arrives. Finally, draft a backup plan in case the task doesn't get done in the scheduled slot. Write down all of these details on a piece of paper, then post it someplace you can always see it as a reminder of how your day is supposed to go.

Scheduling helps you start your day knowing what you need to do and when you're going to do it, so you don't even have to spend as much energy and willpower racking your brains throughout the day, agonizing over which important task you need to complete next. With a schedule, you get to simply follow a clear time-and-motion guide: For a particular time frame, there's a particular action you're directed to do. This will allow you to smoothly and efficiently go from one task to another throughout the day.

Again, the absence of downtime for constructive thought ends up helping you here.

Scheduling also allows you to visualize things such that you can see pockets of time within the day in which you can insert certain activities. For example, you've identified that you have a morning meeting from 10:00 AM to 11:00 AM. Based on that, you see that your 8:00 AM to 10:00 AM slot is actually free and is time you could use accomplishing tasks rather than just waiting for the meeting to start. So to maximize your morning, schedule a task that you estimate will take about two hours to complete for that time slot.

By scheduling, you also get to appreciate just how much time you can afford to spend on a task. You'll be prevented from procrastinating when you see there's a danger of the completion of one task eating away at a time frame you've set for another activity.

In summary, there are several strategies that'll help you start your day already wearing full armor against procrastination. First, plan to have no more zero days so that you're never stagnant and will develop the work habit in your system. Second, use self-interrogation techniques to help you kick-start your motivation to work on your intended tasks.

Third, use the Ivy Lee method to prioritize and accomplish six important tasks for each day. Finally, write down a detailed schedule of your day's activities. Using these strategies to structure your day, you'll surely be giving procrastination a difficult time as it tries to derail you from achieving your goals.

Takeaways:

- This chapter is about how to structure your day to prevent procrastination. Will it work every time, every day? No, but you stand a much better chance when you engage in these exercises than when you don't. Procrastination leaps on you when you have idle time and when you're unengaged. Scheduling and structuring prevents this and attempts to take the decision out of your hands entirely.

- The first step in scheduling is more about how to approach your schedule and day structure. Namely, pledge to yourself to have no more "zero days" where a zero day is a day which you've let slip by without doing anything to achieve your goal. You can also substitute an hour, week, or a minute in place of a day. In any case, having the intention to just act in every time segment will help prevent procrastination.

- Self-interrogation questions can also help you when you're on the cusp of procrastinating. If you ask yourself a certain set of questions, you are able to immediately take a step and break through inertia. The questions are: What is one thing I can do right now? What are my top three priorities today? How can I make this easier for me to follow through? And what will go wrong if I don't try to persevere?

- The Ivy Lee method has been shown to prevent procrastination by simply leaving no room for it. It consists of nailing down your priorities each day, and starting only from the top of the list each day.

- Finally, truly scheduling everything into your agenda works because it lets you visually understand what needs to be done. This effect can be further enhanced if you schedule, along with the task itself, where you shall perform it, what resources are needed, and when it shall be done. The more details and specificity, the better.

Chapter 7. Get Off Your Butt

"The only difference between success and failure is the ability to take action."
—Alexander Graham Bell

In this chapter, I wanted to cover one of procrastination's biggest enemies: the immediate moment. Of course, we know procrastination to be the devil on our shoulders that suggests that we will be totally fine if we push what we should do until another moment, and then another, and then another, and then a few more after the next four. You get the idea.

What is it that makes us want to say "I'll get to it later!" in the hopes that it will disappear forever? Whatever it is, this chapter is aimed at just getting started as a way to break inertia.

10-10-10

Thinking in terms of 10-10-10 is an applied way to think into the future, and it is a common theme of this book.

The next time you feel you're about to give in to a temptation, stop and ask yourself how you will feel 10 minutes, 10 hours, and 10 days from now.

This rule may not seem all that powerful, but it's effective because it forces you to think specifically about your future self and to see how your actions are going to affect yourself in the future—for better or worse. A lot of times, we may know that we are losing willpower or doing something harmful in the moment, but that's not enough to stop us from doing it because we don't have any connection to our future self that will have to deal with the consequences.

This rule quickly creates that connection, and that can make the difference between a success or failure of discipline.

Why time intervals of 10 minutes, hours, and days? Because that helps you realize how short-term a pleasure is relative to its long-term consequences. At 10 minutes, you might be feeling good, with perhaps just the initial bit of shame creeping in. After 10 hours, you'll feel mostly shame a regret. 10 days later, you might be consumed by regret, having realized some of the negative consequences that your decision or action has had on your pursuit of your long-term goals.

On the other hand, you might apply this rule and realize that a lapse in following through now won't make a difference 10 days into the future. If that's the case, then perhaps you can indulge a bit without guilt or shame. This is a book about procrastination, but attempting to eliminate it completely will never work, so some strategic flexibility is sometimes required.

Imagine that you apply this rule when deciding whether or not to skip a workout to go to dinner with coworkers. If you've just begun exercising and haven't built it into a consistent habit yet, your decision to skip a single workout might increase the odds of skipping future workouts, or ceasing to work out altogether.

How will you feel in 10 minutes, hours, and days? 10 minutes—good, with a slight twinge of regret, as you can still taste the lasagna or ice cream. The pleasure is still tangible. 10 hours—almost entirely regret, as the pleasure is gone and fleeting, and your diet has been soundly broken. 10 days—100% regret, because the broken discipline is now completely meaningless and but a faint memory. The lasagna does not have a lasting benefit, but it does have a lasting cost.

On the other hand, if exercising is already a consistent and enjoyable habit for you, then imagining how you'll feel 10 days from now will quickly show you that one skipped workout isn't harmful to your long-term discipline or goals.

And when you're not swayed by this rule, or your dilemma of willpower is extra difficult, you can add a final question for yourself: How will breaking willpower now affect you in 10 weeks, or even longer-term? You might want to change the parameters to 10 weeks if you're mostly engaged in longer-term decisions and tasks.

In this process, it's crucial to be honest with yourself and wary of your own abilities to rationalize and make excuses. For example, you may have tried to quit an addictive habit many times in the past, only to fail and eventually reinforce the harmful behavior. If you have a history of falling into bad habits after a single lapse in discipline, then an honest assessment of how you would feel after 10 days or 10 weeks will tell you that you simply can't afford a lapse in discipline now, if you're going to achieve your long-term goals. It wasn't an exception or justified in that one circumstance—it is a reflection of your character, for better or worse.

Without that honesty and ability to recognize your own rationalizing and excuses for what they are, applying this rule may be a futile exercise.

But wait—there's more significance to the 10-10-10 Rule. You could call this the 10-Minute Correlate.

If you want to do something that amounts to procrastination—something negative, harmful, or detrimental to your follow-through—wait at least 10 minutes before doing it.

It's simple and leaves no room for debate or excuses. When you feel an urge, force yourself to wait for 10 minutes before giving in to whatever the urge is. If you're still craving it after 10 minutes, then have it. Or wait 10 more minutes because you've already done it and survived just fine. By simply choosing to wait, you remove the "immediate" from immediate gratification, thereby building discipline and improving your decision-making.

Similarly, if you want to quit something beneficial, wait just 10 more minutes. It's the same thought process applied in a different way. 10 minutes is nothing, so you easily can wait or continue for that amount of time. Then, if you do it once, it's easy to repeat, isn't it? In other words, say to yourself "just 10 minutes more of willpower" each time you reach a fork in the road.

Another benefit of this rule is the purposeful escalation of good habits. If you've forced yourself to do something productive for 10 minutes, you might end up doing it for 15 or even 20 minutes more. Next time, your tolerance will build such that you're more immune to temptation and distraction—the following time you might continue for an extra six or seven minutes.

Every time you feel distracted, just exercise willpower for a few minutes longer and you'll steadily follow through better with each escalation. At some iteration of "just 10 minutes more," you'll reach a point of momentum, and that's often enough to carry you for hours.

The 40–70 Rule

Can you actually be too prepared? Is this causing you to procrastinate?

Former U.S. Secretary of State Colin Powell has a rule of thumb about coming to a point of action. He says that any time you face a hard choice, you should have *no less* than 40% and *no more* than 70% of the information you need to make that decision. In that range, you have enough information to make an informed choice, but not so much intelligence that you lose your resolve and simply stay abreast of the situation.

If you have less than 40% of the information you need, you're essentially shooting from the hip. You don't know quite enough to move forward and will probably make a lot of mistakes. Conversely, if you chase down more data until you get more than 70% of what you need (and it's unlikely that you'll truly need anything above this level), you could get overwhelmed and uncertain. The opportunity may have passed you by, and someone else may have beaten you by starting already.

This is the zone of procrastination—you want 100% information, and although it's never possible, it's a zone of safety.

But in that sweet spot between 40% and 70%, you have enough to go on and let your intuition guide your decisions. In the context of Colin Powell, this is where effective leaders are made: the people who have instincts that point in the right direction are who will lead their organization to success. This is also where you should battle procrastination before it becomes too late. You should feel a certain amount of uncertainty, or even lack of confidence—it's natural, and anything else is an unrealistic expectation. More often than not, what you are searching for will only be gained through *beginning*.

We can replace the word "information" with other motivators: 40–70% of experience, 40–70% reading or learning, 40–70% confidence, or 40–70% of planning. While we're taking action, we learn, gain confidence, and gain momentum.

When you try to achieve more than 70% information (or confidence, experience, etc.), your lack of speed can destroy your momentum or stem your interest, effectively meaning nothing's going to happen. There is a high likelihood of gaining nothing further from surpassing this threshold.

For example, let's say you're opening up a cocktail bar, which involves buying a lot of different types of liquor. You're going to wait until you're 100% ready with your liquor before opening.

You can't expect to have absolutely all the liquor you will ever need when the doors are ready to open. It's impossible to able to serve any drink that a customer orders.

So, applying this rule, you'd wait until you had at least 40% of your available inventory prepared. This would establish momentum.

Then, if you could get more than half of what you need, you'd be in pretty good shape to open. You might not be able to make absolutely every drink in the bartender's guide, but you'll have enough on-hand to cover the staple drinks with a couple of variations. If you have around 50–60% inventory, you're more than ready.

When the remaining inventory arrives, you'll already be in action and can just incorporate that new inventory into your offerings. If you waited until you had 70% or more inventory, you could find yourself stuck in neutral for longer than you wanted to be.

This way of thinking leads to more action than not. Waiting until you have 40% of what you need to make a move isn't a way of staying inside your comfort zone—you're actively planning what you need to do to get out, which is just fine (as long as it's not over-planning).

Tiny Steps

Very few people want to go to work when it's raining cats and dogs outside.

It's an enormous burden to overcome mentally. You'll get soaked, your shoes and socks will be puddles, and you'll freeze from head to toe. Oh, and your only umbrella is broken. It's such a burden that you don't even want to go through the motions of getting dressed and putting on your boots. You feel defeated before you even get started.

Sometimes a horrendously rainy day can feel just like trying to be productive.

When we're faced with huge tasks that feel insurmountable, it's like looking through a window out at the rain. It's such an obstacle that everything feels impossible and pointless. We drag our feet, discourage ourselves, and bitterly complain the whole time.

But that's the wrong way to look at the tasks on our plates.

A single huge task, such as "finish the 200-page report," can certainly sound imposing, if not impossible. However, what if you were to break that monumental task up into tiny, individual, easy tasks you could get to work on immediately?

For example: preparing the template, finding the first three sources, creating a bibliography, outlining 500 words of the first section, and so on. Actually, it can go much smaller yet: choosing the fonts, writing the chapter titles, organizing the desk, formatting the document, or writing just one sentence. The smaller, the better, otherwise you're starting each day staring at the equivalent of a rainy day.

One of the biggest hurdles to productivity is looking at tasks as huge, inseparable boulders. It's intimidating and discouraging, and when those emotions arise, it's tough to avoid procrastinating because tackling a boulder is a tough sell. Unfortunately, this is a habit that plagues most people. They see only massive boulders and allow themselves to get emotionally thrown off track.

Break up your big tasks into smaller tasks, and keep repeating until the tasks you have before you are so easy you can do them within a few minutes. Create small, manageable chunks that will be psychologically uplifting and acceptable, and you'll kick your production up instantly. Make your to-do list as long and articulated as possible, with as many small tasks as you can list. A pebble is something you can do instantly, without any effort, and even with little thought.

Productivity is nothing without action, and action is much easier with something simple and easy to warm up with. Small steps can take you to the top of the hill and let you roll down the other side to seize momentum. They help you break the inertia that leads you to passivity and inaction.

Let's take an example that we're all familiar with: working out. You want to lose 100 pounds, a hefty goal.

If you go into the gym every day thinking that you want to lose 100 pounds, you're probably going to fail. It's a huge, enormous boulder of a goal. It might sound grand to proclaim, but in reality, it is going to be very hard to stick to because of how unbelievable it sounds.

You won't see much progress on a daily or even weekly basis, and you will understandably become discouraged. It's too much to face at once, like the rainy day from the beginning of the chapter. What if you approached your weight loss goal by breaking it into small, manageable increments (goals) and tasks?

This might look something like setting a reasonable weekly weight loss goal, creating daily goals of eating specific foods (and not eating others), and drinking water every hour. Eat 100 fewer calories per meal. Go on walks after each meal. Drink only half your soda. Eat five fewer fries each meal. Cook once a week. Buy the low-calorie version of snacks.

If you hit your weekly weight loss goal and successfully drink water every hour, it is far easier to stay motivated and focused. Meeting your smaller, weekly goal will give you a sense of accomplishment, whereas making an insignificant dent in your total goal (100 pounds) will only make you feel discouraged, and as if the task ahead is too great to achieve.

These are small tasks that, if done consistently and correctly, will lead to your overall goal of losing 100 pounds.

These small victories will encourage and motivate you—and so it is with tasks, productivity, and procrastination. Don't underestimate the power of small victories.

Banish Excuses

People use excuses to postpone taking action and to procrastinate. Most excuses, however, are poppycock—invalid, rubbish, and rationalized. Excuses are our subconscious protecting us from our fears. It is your automatic pilot saying, "Danger! This might not go well! Let me save you!" Let's look at some common excuses people use to procrastinate.

Now is not the right time. Related variations: *I can't do X until... I can't do X unless...* True. There is never a perfect time for anything. There are mediocre times and terrible times, but rarely are there perfect times. Stop putting conditions around your ability to work. All you are doing is creating a psychological gatekeeper for yourself that is detrimental.

Timing is everything—that's actually not true. Timing just *is*. There is no good time for a crisis, but they happen anyway. When trying to be productive, rarely is there an obvious time that is better than another. It's just a lie we tell ourselves. There are always going to be obstacles to overcome and hassles to manage. In fact, 99% of the time you want to do something, the timing will be mediocre, 1% the timing will be truly terrible, and that's it. There should never be any expectations of having perfect timing.

When is the right time to travel? When is the right time to get married? When is the right time to have a child? When is the right time to quit? You know the answer to these questions.

For instance, there is never a perfect time to sell a house. The housing market is unpredictable, and various rates are subject to change overnight. You also don't know what bids you will receive and if anyone will even view your home. On the other hand, there are some objectively horrible times to sell a house, like when a main employer in town lays off 50% of its workforce and interest rates take a 10% rise.

Many of us wish timing was something we had more control over, but the fact remains that we rarely get to choose when something happens to us. We do, however, get to choose when we take action. If you find yourself questioning this, the time to act has already arrived.

I don't know where to start. You do; the problem is you think you need an entire plan before starting. People need to stop expecting to see a clear path through to the end before they even begin.

Here is the secret: You don't need to know where you will finish to know where to start. The number one college major for students entering university in the U.S. is *undecided*. Most 18-year-olds are not able to articulate what they want to study that will lead to a lifelong career. However, we encourage young people to get to college soon after high school. "Don't wait too long. Don't get too many responsibilities." During the four (or five) years they are on campus, most students declare a major and start working toward a degree that will eventually lead to employment.

We think nothing of this process; however, so many times in adulthood people become paralyzed because they don't see a clear finish line. Doing something today with what you have today is the key. Stop researching, stop agonizing, stop wasting time, and start doing. Do what you can do right now at this very moment, and you can figure out the next steps after. You probably know your next steps, however small they may be.

The blank page or the blank screen is the writer's nightmare. It does not matter if the writer is a middle schooler with a book report due or Stephen King. The blank page is terrifying. And yet, all who eventually produced something to fill that paper or screen had to stop reading the book, stop researching the topic, stop planning out the flow, and just start writing.

The first words written may not be any good. They may be terrible and need to be changed. But the writer cannot get there if they never write any words down. The way to start writing is simple: start writing.

Focusing on the end product, a hardback with a glossy cover, isn't the goal at the beginning. A beginning is the goal. After you start, the rest will take care of itself because you will know what needs to be done to get you to the next step, and then the one after that.

I'm not good enough. Shockingly, that just might be true. A person may really want to do something, but they might not be good enough. What is the answer to that dilemma? You can *become* good enough.

Sometimes the only way to get what you want is to shift into a growth mindset and start working. Make sure that this time next year, you know more than you know now and that your skills are better than they are now. If you are willing to take the first steps, what you need will follow.

When you feel like you are not good enough, you might need to reframe it just a bit to "I'm not good enough at this moment." After all, why would anyone have the expectation that they would be good enough at something without practice, work, and a significant amount of time? You simply cannot have the expectation of instant, or even preemptive excellence. If you never start, you will never be good enough, and you will have prophesized your own future.

Learning a musical instrument is an illustrative example. When people say they aren't musical before picking up an instrument, it makes little sense, doesn't it? If learning to play the piano is your goal, then you can certainly make it happen. You would have to start back at that beginning middle C, but with lessons, practice, patience, and perseverance.

Anyone, including you, can learn to play the piano. Who knows? Perhaps you could eventually become a keyboard player for a Queen cover band. Just because you are not good enough now does not mean you cannot become good enough eventually.

Combating excuses is difficult because of our overwhelming need for self-protection. We may not even realize when we are using defense mechanisms to procrastinate, but chances are if you find yourself justifying a lack of action, it's a defense mechanism.

Takeaways:

- Getting off your butt might be the very essence of conquering procrastination. Procrastination's mortal enemy is the immediate, present moment. So how do we seize that?

- First, by utilizing the 10-10-10 Rule. Consider how you'll feel in 10 minutes, hours, and days if you procrastinate. Visualize your future self (again) and feel the consequences. There may not actually be any, in which case you can feel free to relax a bit. Going cold turkey on procrastinating is nearly impossible, so you can design in some flexibility from time to time.

- Utilize the 40-70 Rule as popularized by Colin Powell. This rule states the following: You only need between 40% and 70% of the information, confidence, time, or preparation that you think you do. Anything else is just spinning your wheels and procrastinating, and 100% of what you want is impossible from the starting line. So take action at 70%, at worst, because things won't improve by simply waiting longer.

- Tiny steps are the best steps. Large tasks looks intimidating and impossible. But when you break each boulder down into small pebbles which can be taken care of instantaneously and effortlessly, then you have a chance of building momentum and taking care of what needs to be done in short order.
- We are full of excuses for the protection of our ego. But of course, excuses are detrimental to your working spirit. It's important to realize that these excuses are largely fabrications. Not right now— there is never a perfect time. I'm not good enough—no, but you can become good enough. I don't know where to start—start with what you can do right now, not only with an ultimate end point in mind.

Summary Guide

Chapter 1. Procrastination: The Ancient Foe

- Procrastination has been around far longer than you or I. The term "procrastination" was derived from the Latin *pro*, meaning "forward, forth, or in favor of" and *crastinus*, meaning "of tomorrow." In everyday terms, it's when you put off something unpleasant, usually in pursuit of something more pleasurable or enjoyable.

- The pleasure principle is important to understand in the context of procrastination. Our brains have a constant civil war brewing inside; the impulsive and largely subconscious lizard brain wants immediate pleasure at the expense of the slower prefrontal cortex, which makes rational decisions. The prefrontal cortex makes the unpopular decisions which procrastination is not a fan of, while the lizard brain makes decisions that lead to dopamine and adrenaline being produced. It may seem like a losing battle, but the key to battling procrastination is being able to regulate our impulses and drives—though not suppress them.

- It's been found that there are nine specific traits associated with procrastination. They include: (1) inhibition, (2) self-monitoring, (3) planning and organization, (4) activity shifting, (5) task initiation, (6) task monitoring, (7) emotional control, (8) working memory, and (9) general orderliness. Generally, deficiencies in any of these nine traits will make an individual more susceptible to procrastination. To beat procrastination, we must perform one of the hardest tasks of all: thinking about one's own thinking.

Chapter 2. Danger: Warning Signs

- This chapter is about the warning signs that procrastination is imminent. There are far too many to name, but there are a few common types that can be helpful to articulate and then diagnose in yourself. They come in the context that there are generally five different types of procrastinators: (1) thrill-seeker, (2) avoider, (3) indecisive, (4) perfectionist, and (5) busy. Each type has its own triggers, like the feeling of adrenaline and risk, avoiding rejection, and feeling overwhelmed. They can generally be grouped into two general kinds of procrastination triggers: action-based and mental/emotion-based.
- No matter the warning signs for you, they might not matter if you are simply an impulsive person who disregards rational thought and lives in the moment. This might sound positive, but it is not a pretty sight. Four traits make up impulsivity: urgency (I must do this right now), lack of premeditation (I

don't know how this will affect me later), lack of perseverance (I'm tired of this, what else is there to do?), and sensation-seeking (Oh, that feels better than what I am currently doing). The more elevated your levels, the more impulsive and procrastinating you will be.

- A helpful method for defeating procrastination is called HALT, and it stands for Hunger, Anger, Loneliness, or Tiredness. When you are facing a fork in the road in regards to persevering or procrastinating, ask yourself if any of the HALT factors are present. If any are, understand that you are already predisposed to making a poor decision and try to regulate your thoughts.

Chapter 3: Anti-Procrastination Mindsets

- Procrastination may be a reflection of battling biological forces, and we can swing the battle in our favor if we use some of the mindset tactics in this chapter. Fear is an understated underlying cause for procrastination.

- The first such tactic is to understand how Newton's three laws of physics can apply to procrastination. Viewing your productivity (or lack thereof) as an equation is helpful, because it allows you to think through the variables present in your life and learn how to manipulate them. First, an object at rest tends to stay at rest, while an object in motion tends to stay in motion (the first step is the hardest step). Next, the amount of work produced is a product of the focus and the force that is applied toward it (focus your efforts intentionally). Finally, for every action, there is an equal and opposite reaction (take inventory of the productive and unproductive forces present in your life).

- Another factor in procrastination is the paradox of choice, wherein choices and options are actually detrimental because they cause indecision and plague us with doubt. They might even cause us to act like Buridan's donkey and proverbially starve to death between two dishes of food. To combat this, get into the habit of setting a time limit on your decisions, making matters black and white, aiming to become satisficed, and immediately picking a default option.

- Finally, finding the right motivation can be important. It's not that you should only do things that you feel motivation for, but rather, you can find bits and pieces of what motivates you and what you value in everything you do. It's just a matter of looking.

Chapter 4: Psychological Tactics

- Sometimes it's necessary to trick ourselves into doing what we don't want to. In fact, that's a primary aspect of improving and practicing anything. We are momentarily seduced by the benefit or end result to the point where we can grin and bear the present pain.
- Many of us think we can only work when are in the mood for it, or when

inspiration strikes us. That is a losing battle. Don't rely on your mood to get you where you want to go. Instead, think the opposite way: Once you begin action, your mood will follow. Forgive yourself for procrastinating, because that prevents you from a negative spiral and giving up altogether.

- Understand and tame omission bias. This is when you realize that it's easy to feel the impact from doing something, but not the impact from skipping something. This is about more than awareness; you can battle omission bias with proactive visualization of the bad future you are creating. That will kick you into gear.

- Finally, visualize your future self. Most of us suffer from *temporal myopia,* which is when you as nearsighted with regards to time. Specifically, you don't think about your future self; when you can effectively visualize your future self in excruciating detail, you are more aware of what you need to do and more impacted by it—because you recognize that you are your own future!

Chapter 5: Strategic Planning

- Even though we know procrastination is always lurking, we can't always fight it, no matter how close attention we pay. That's why it pays to structure your day and work to avoid procrastination completely. At least you'll give yourself a much better fighting chance.
- First, you can use the STING method, by which you select one task, time yourself, ignore everything else, opt for no breaks, and give yourself a reward. It's the act of willful ignorance that makes STING so powerful. This is a scary concept, but once you resolve to only juggle one thing at a time, you'll be happy to report that the world didn't end.
- Secondly, rather than being pressured to achieve the end product as a whole, you can choose to focus on the process so you're better able to manage smaller chunks of work at a time. Just imagine

the small tasks you have to do without thinking about the mountain you are tackling.

- Third, you can use your knowledge of the procrastination equation to your advantage by increasing both success expectancy and task value while decreasing reward delay and impulsiveness. You can manipulate each of these variables to increase your motivation and momentum toward productivity.

- Fourth, you can make your hated tasks compete against each other such that you'll tend to procrastinate on your most hated tasks by still being productive as you work on your less hated activities.

- Finally, you can bundle temptations. This essentially means to simultaneously satisfy the hedonist in your current self and the prudence of your future self. Make both happy at the same time by pairing unpleasant tasks with sought-after pleasures.

Chapter 6: Structuring Against Procrastination

- This chapter is about how to structure your day to prevent procrastination. Will it work every time, every day? No, but you stand a much better chance when you engage in these exercises than when you don't. Procrastination leaps on you when you have idle time and when you're unengaged. Scheduling and structuring prevents this and attempts to take the decision out of your hands entirely.

- The first step in scheduling is more about how to approach your schedule and day structure. Namely, pledge to yourself to have no more "zero days" where a zero day is a day which you've let slip by without doing anything to achieve your goal. You can also substitute an hour, week, or a minute in place of a day. In any case, having the intention to just act in every time segment will help prevent procrastination.

- Self-interrogation questions can also help you when you're on the cusp of procrastinating. If you ask yourself a certain set of questions, you are able to immediately take a step and break through inertia. The questions are: What is one thing I can do right now? What are my top three priorities today? How can I make this easier for me to follow through? And what will go wrong if I don't try to persevere?
- The Ivy Lee method has been shown to prevent procrastination by simply leaving no room for it. It consists of nailing down your priorities each day, and starting only from the top of the list each day.
- Finally, truly scheduling everything into your agenda works because it lets you visually understand what needs to be done. This effect can be further enhanced if you schedule, along with the task itself, where you shall perform it, what resources are needed, and when it shall be done. The more details and specificity, the better.

Chapter 7. Get Off Your Butt

- Getting off your butt might be the very essence of conquering procrastination. Procrastination's mortal enemy is the immediate, present moment. So how do we seize that?

- First, by utilizing the 10-10-10 Rule. Consider how you'll feel in 10 minutes, hours, and days if you procrastinate. Visualize your future self (again) and feel the consequences. There may not actually be any, in which case you can feel free to relax a bit. Going cold turkey on procrastinating is nearly impossible, so you can design in some flexibility from time to time.

- Utilize the 40-70 Rule as popularized by Colin Powell. This rule states the following: You only need between 40% and 70% of the information, confidence, time, or preparation that you think you do. Anything else is just spinning your wheels and procrastinating, and 100% of what you want is impossible from the starting line. So take action at 70%, at worst, because things won't improve by simply waiting longer.

- Tiny steps are the best steps. Large tasks looks intimidating and impossible. But when you break each boulder down into small pebbles which can be taken care of instantaneously and effortlessly, then you have a chance of building momentum and taking care of what needs to be done in short order.
- We are full of excuses for the protection of our ego. But of course, excuses are detrimental to your working spirit. It's important to realize that these excuses are largely fabrications. Not right now—there is never a perfect time. I'm not good enough—no, but you can become good enough. I don't know where to start—start with what you can do right now, not only with an ultimate end point in mind.

40263035R00130

Outsmart your lazy and undisciplined tendencies.
Become a productivity machine and achieve your
goals in record time.

Procrastination is the monster that we are always
running from, but not always successfully. It lurks
around every corner, and can completely sabotage
your life. But you can learn to defeat it every time.

The Science of Overcoming Procrastination is a
deep dive into our tendency to push things until
the last minute possible. It uncovers the biological
and evolutionary science behind procrastination,
and how we can beat these instinctual drives to
triumph in our career and personal life. A plethora
of studies are analyzed and put into illuminating
contexts.

Patrick King is a Social Interaction Specialist based
in San Francisco, California. He runs Patrick King
Consulting and is an internationally bestselling
author. He teaches social, conversation, and
communication skills, which he deems the "greasy
crowbars" of life because they simply give you
access. More frequently than not, you can find
Patrick training for his next road race or fronting a
1980's cover band.

ISBN 9781718851122

90000 >

9 781718 851122